D1571672

WOLFE&HIGGINS

MASTER ARCHITECTS OF
THE SPANISH REVIVAL

by Krista Van Laan

Published by Archives & Architecture LLC

2017

Krista Van Z

Published by
Archives & Architecture, LLC
PO Box 1332
San José, CA 95109

Orders: **www.archivesandarchitecture.com**

To learn more about Frank Delos Wolfe, go to **www.frankdeloswolfe.com**

Editor: Marcy Van Laan

Printed in the USA
Signature Book Printing, www.sbpbooks.com

Van Laan, Krista
Wolfe & Higgins: Master Architects of the Spanish Revival

ISBN 978-0-692-58098-1
Library of Congress Control Number: 2015919093

WOLFE&HIGGINS

MASTER ARCHITECTS OF
THE SPANISH REVIVAL

Contents

Foreword

As a California Bay Area native, a licensed architect, and a practicing architectural historian, I know something of Bay Area architects of the past. But local references are rare, and too often I'm at a loss to recognize or properly appreciate the bodies of work of the architects who came before me. My colleagues and I have, over the years, pieced together a working knowledge base of the architects who designed buildings in the South Bay Area and the Monterey Bay Region, but it's merely an in-house list—nothing particularly interesting or complete.

Enter Krista Van Laan, who has the passion to pursue the historical research, hunt down existing architectural works, and uncover the stories behind the facts. She also has the writing skill to spin tales fascinating enough for the general public, while still providing substantiated data for professionals.

I absolutely loved *Frank Delos Wolfe: California Prairie Architecture*, written by Van Laan two years ago about a well-loved and creative local designer. Van Laan added a human layer to the physical story of wood, bricks, stucco, and tile, each house receiving an engaging vignette that I read in relaxed enjoyment. When I learned Van Laan would be writing another architectural history book, I was delighted. When I learned that she would be writing about the next generation of Wolfe-family buildings, I was filled with even more anticipation.

Van Laan's new book spotlights an architectural firm, Wolfe & Higgins, that is previously under-reported yet absolutely deserving of the attention. Wolfe & Higgins designed building after building in the South Bay Area with talent and originality.

I was aware of the firm's work in an abstract way, but until I read this book, I hadn't fully grasped the breadth, depth, and quality of Wolfe & Higgins's designs. This is a comprehensive book, full of superb recent color photos and sharp black-and-white historic photos, along with blueprint images, historic postcards, and other historic images that provide a backdrop for the stories. The narratives about the owners and the architects are addictive snippets of life in the early twentieth century, and every page of *Wolfe & Higgins: Master Architects of the Spanish Revival* reveals architectural compositions of enduring warmth.

The elements illustrated in the book—arched focal windows, carved roof brackets, red-tile roofs, ornate doorway surrounds, and sky-lit spaces—represent both a specific time in history and a future of timeless elegance. The book is everything I'd hoped and expected it would be.

Leslie A.G. Dill
Architect and Architectural Historian

Preface

The last ten years of my life have been consumed by the doings of a local architect who died nearly a century ago. In 2006, I bought a remarkable house in San José, California—a 1921 Prairie-style creation that brought to mind the Oak Park, Illinois buildings of Frank Lloyd Wright. My house was the work of San José architect Frank Delos Wolfe, an astoundingly prolific and forward-thinking designer who was responsible for well over one thousand buildings during an architectural career that lasted from 1888 to 1926. Eight of those buildings are today on the National Register of Historic Places.

My interest in my house launched a period of intense research into the work of Wolfe, in particular the Prairie buildings that dot the cityscape of my adopted home, San José. In 2012, I chaired a city-wide homes tour of Wolfe's Prairie architecture for the Preservation Action Council of San José, and in 2014, I published *Frank Delos Wolfe: California Prairie Architecture*, a book on—what else?—the Prairie architecture of Frank Delos Wolfe. Since the book was released, I have gone all over Northern California to talk about Wolfe's work and have been pleased and gratified at the interest shown in this topic. Wolfe's architecture speaks to a wide audience.

When I started that book, I was aware of only two key periods of Frank Wolfe's career—his years as part of the architectural firm of Wolfe & McKenzie, and his years as an independent architect, during which he launched his Prairie designs. From 1899 through 1910, Wolfe partnered with Charles McKenzie to produce unique eclectic residential designs that are found in historic neighborhoods throughout Northern California. After the Wolfe & McKenzie partnership dissolved, Frank Wolfe introduced the first of his Frank Lloyd Wright-inspired Prairie School designs. The demand was so high that Wolfe's son Carl joined his business and the firm produced buildings in this style until the late 1910s when its popularity waned. Today, more than one hundred years later, Prairie School architecture seems to be more popular than ever, and many of Frank Wolfe's California Prairies are as well-loved as Frank Lloyd Wright's Midwestern counterparts. Most of these striking Bay Area homes are still standing and have devoted owners who appreciate their unique value.

Prairie was the style I associated with Frank Wolfe and I thought that when the national interest in Prairie School architecture wound down, that he did, too. I was aware that at the end of 1917, he entered a new partnership with architect William Ernest Higgins, but I had yet to learn about the firm's work.

In fact, the prolific Wolfe was responsible for introducing yet another architectural style to the Santa Clara Valley. With William Ernest Higgins, Wolfe specialized in Spanish Revival (also known as Spanish Colonial Revival, or Spanish Eclectic) architecture, often utilizing the Churrigueresque style that featured elaborate sculptural decoration, particularly around the entrance of the building. Spanish Revival was a style that had gained popularity in California because of San Diego's Panama-California Exposition of 1915-1917. Wolfe & Higgins were among the first Northern California architects to work in this style, which was soon to become emblematic of California architecture. Although Wolfe & Higgins were also locally known for other Revival styles such as Dutch Colonial and Tudor, it was Spanish Revival, with its low-pitched tile roofs, arches, and rich ornamentation that became the mainstay of their business and remained so until the very end. When Wolfe died in 1926, his son Carl took over the partnership and the firm continued to work almost exclusively in Spanish Revival until Carl's death in 1931.

What was startling, as I began to research the work of this period, was to discover that some of my favorite buildings in San José—in fact, some of the most recognizable buildings in the area—were Spanish Revival buildings designed by Wolfe & Higgins. Soon, these buildings seemed to be everywhere I looked. I eventually amassed a list of well over 500 houses, commercial buildings, and schools done by the firm of Wolfe & Higgins from 1918 to 1931, and have spent much time determining which of them are still standing. (Less than half, as it turns out.) There are many more yet-to-be-identified buildings—possibly hundreds more—that are almost certainly also the work of Wolfe & Higgins.

This book shows not only the best of that work, but it also emphasizes the sheer quantity of Wolfe & Higgins's portfolio. Of the more than 500 buildings for which Wolfe & Higgins were responsible during its fourteen years in business, over 130 are shown in this book, giving a sense of just how prolific the firm was.

San José alone has block after block of distinctive Spanish Revival one-story houses in the Wolfe & Higgins style, so many that it can be said to be a significant architectural style representative of the city. A number of real estate developers and builders in the 1920s—including Tony Maderis, A. Clyde Alexander, Alfred Jones, and Adolph Goldstein—used Wolfe & Higgins as their architects, often exclusively. These developers would hire Wolfe & Higgins to design their personal residences, and also have the firm provide designs for spec houses, which they would turn around and sell or use to populate new developments. The Wolfe & Higgins designs were popular with both builders and buyers; the same design was often replicated, sometimes with minor modifications, throughout a neighborhood or around the city.

Spanish Revival houses continued to be built well into the 1930s, after the end of the Wolfe & Higgins firm; in addition, kit home catalogs from companies such as Pacific Ready-Cut Homes offered a number of beautiful Spanish Revival homes. All of these factors can make it hard to definitely state if a house is a Wolfe & Higgins design if I don't have corroborating documentation. Although in many cases I can make an educated guess, I have avoided doing that in this book unless there is strong evidence to indicate that a design is that of Wolfe & Higgins. I will only say that if you live in San José in a one-story stucco house built in the 1920s with a low-pitched tile roof and three arched windows with twisted spiral columns, there is a very strong chance that your home was designed by Wolfe & Higgins.

I have found the firm's work not only in San José, where their office was located, but in San Francisco, in San Mateo County, and in many cities throughout the Bay Area. One of their most famous works, the Venetian Court, is in Capitola, and appears on postcards and souvenir items as a symbol of that beautiful beach town.

Identifying and cataloging the work of a prolific architect like Frank Wolfe are not trivial tasks. It can take an enormous amount of time to locate a building whose only reference might be a brief mention in an old newspaper. I start by looking through newspapers and old builders' magazines for mentions of Wolfe's work, and it is in those that I find most of my leads.

The next step is to try to find the building. The references in the builders' magazines are often vague, citing a general location rather than a specific address. Street names change over the years, as do street numbers. Tracking down the building based on a client's name has its own set of problems, from misspellings, to clients moving frequently, to the fact that many of the customers of Wolfe & Higgins had multiple properties, making it hard to identify the one I'm looking for. It can take many days to identify just one building and determine if it is still standing, and I am working with a list of about 500.

While many of the Wolfe & Higgins residences still exist, nearly all of their commercial buildings have been demolished, unfortunately. When I discover one still standing, it's a cause for celebration; greater celebration still if the building has not been modified beyond recognition. The same is true of the schools—it's rare to find a school that is still standing. One of the biggest thrills of the Wolfe & Higgins hunt was discovering that the last project Carl Wolfe worked on, the St. Helena Grammar School, is still standing today, and most surprising, still in use as an elementary school and still true to its original form. This beautiful building is shown in the last pages of this book.

Although other local architects worked in the Spanish Revival style, none made it their signature style as Wolfe & Higgins did and none, in Santa Clara County at least, seems to have adopted it as early as did Wolfe & Higgins. As he had been earlier in his career, Wolfe was ahead of the pack in his desire to try out new architectural styles. While Frank Wolfe was still alive, the firm produced memorable work such as the Curtner-Richards house (a San José City Landmark), the Gertrude Gardiner apartment building at Stanford, the Venetian Court in Capitola, and spectacular residences for clients including Grace Spencer Hall, Robert Wright, and Frank and Caroline Dreischmeyer in San José.

A major benefit of this project was that it helped me uncover the work of William Ernest Higgins. Although Higgins came from a locally prominent family whose fascinating story is told in these pages, there has not been a lot known about him or his work. In 2014, I was lucky to discover that the Wilmer and Dorothy Gross house of San José was one of the few designs known to have been done by William Higgins prior to his partnership with Wolfe; my research was instrumental in having it declared a San José City Landmark. The Gross house is an excellent example of the Dutch Colonial Revival style Higgins favored, a style that appears sporadically during the Wolfe & Higgins years. Although Dutch Colonial Revival, popular in the eastern part of the United States, might be the last thing you would expect to see in a historic neighborhood in Santa Clara County, these Higgins-esque houses with their gambrel roofs and elaborate pillared porches made more than one appearance during the Wolfe & Higgins era.

This book also allows me to showcase the abilities of Frank Delos Wolfe's son Carl Jay Wolfe, whose contributions have not been so clearly known to date. Lacking an architect's license, Carl was not declared a partner during his father's lifetime. After the end of World War I, he joined the firm of Wolfe & Higgins as a draftsman, and in 1926, upon Frank Wolfe's death, Carl Wolfe and William Higgins became partners. For the next five years until Carl's premature death in 1931, Carl proved he was a fine architect in his own right, as the firm continued to produce outstanding local works that included the Packard Building, the residence of local political boss Charles Bigley, the San José Woman's Club, and the St. Helena Grammar School.

Like Wolfe's Prairie-style houses, the Wolfe & Higgins-era houses are both beautiful and functional. In 1909, Davis's *Commercial Encyclopedia of the Pacific Northwest* summed up Frank Wolfe when it said: "He is known as a practical designer possessed of much artistic ability." The long-lasting beauty and practical functionality of all of the work Wolfe did continues to impress me. When I visit a Wolfe home, I am always struck by how livable it is for today's modern and demanding homeowners. The firm of Wolfe & Higgins continued to design interiors with wide open spaces and easy traffic flow from room to room, multiple doors and windows, and large closets and bathrooms. In addition to the comfortable interiors, the exteriors are beautiful, with decorative moldings and tiles, arched doors and windows, and wrought iron.

A century later, the Spanish Revival style has not lost its popularity. Today, there is an unprecedented amount of building going on in the San Francisco Bay area to meet the demand for housing. As I pass the build sites for high-density housing and mixed-used development, I notice that almost without exception, the developers' style of choice is Spanish Revival, just as it was in the 1920s when large numbers of developers and builders chose Wolfe & Higgins as their architect. Back then, however, an affordable Spanish Revival small house would include exterior ornamentation done by a master craftsman and a Batchelder-tiled fireplace inside to boot. High-density housing that is intended to accommodate an influx of tech workers in an area where real estate prices continue to skyrocket will hardly allow for such work.

Although Wolfe was very well-known in his time, after his death in 1926, interest in and knowledge of the residential architects of the Santa Clara Valley waned, until no one knew his name. I am pleased to help further public knowledge of the architecture of Frank Delos Wolfe, William Ernest Higgins, and Carl Jay Wolfe. And, as I stated in my last book, I will always be grateful to the work of the late architect George Espinola, who dedicated fifteen years to researching Frank Wolfe. George's 2004 book, *Cottages, Flats, Buildings & Bungalows: 102 Designs from Wolfe & McKenzie, 1907* brought Wolfe's work back to public attention after decades of obscurity.

Some notes:

Those of you who read my 2014 book *Frank Delos Wolfe: California Prairie Architecture* may notice that some dates or references to buildings are different in the two books. The information in this book is the most up-to-date, based on my current knowledge.

All of the work done by the firm of Wolfe & Higgins was in California; therefore, all cities mentioned, unless otherwise specified, are in California.

Although I have done my best to be accurate regarding the years in which these buildings were constructed, there will be times when a date given in this book is the design date rather than the construction date. Sometimes the only available date of record is the year the project was worked on by Wolfe & Higgins, which may not be the same year the building was completed. Some buildings, such as the Woman's Club, were years in the making, and others were built within just a few months of the plans being completed.

During my research into the Wolfe & Higgins era, I was fortunate to find not only some of their original blueprints and specs but also their logo, which was in the Artcraft typeface, a relatively new typeface at that time. I figure that Wolfe & Higgins knew better than anyone else what best represented them, so this book uses Artcraft as its primary typeface.

Wolfe & Higgins
Architects
Realty Building, 19 North Second Street
Phone San Jose 6073
San Jose, California

Acknowledgments

I must thank a great number of people whose contributions have helped with the creation of this book.

Major thanks go to the descendants of the Wolfe and Higgins families, especially for the use of their photographs: Meghan Doe Almeida, Lori Deal, Jane Higgins Hauser, and Anne Wolfe.

I am so grateful to the homeowners and business owners who let me into their beautiful houses. Thank you to Jeanie Alkire and Randy Beaver,

Lisa and Steven Berry, Wendy and Brian Brennan, Larry Camuso and Kirk Wentland, Dr. Chiu-Jung Yuan, Karen and Carl Claras, Jackie and Todd Courtney, Rose Crimi, Patt Curia of the San José Woman's Club, Rick Dunham of Dunham Associates, Syndi and Scott Gemmett, Bernadette DeMao Hunter and Timothy William Hunter, Reverend Sylvia Karuna Lunt of the Center for Spiritual Enlightenment, Sally and Tom Logothetti, Bishop P.J. McGrath, Dick and Marie Munley, Flo and Jim Pleyte, Carol and Clive Pollard, Leslie and Jackson Schwabacher, Joan Talbert and David Lyon, Joe Tate and Yuan Yuan Lu, Carol and John Traub, and Greg and Liz Winslow.

People who have been exceptionally generous with their time and assistance include Judy Everett, Mariam Hovanesian Hansen of the St. Helena Historical Society, Franklin Maggi, Howard Partridge, and Sharlene Van Rooy of the San Benito County Historical Society.

Thanks also go to Bev Blockie, Leslie Dill, Charlene Duval, Carolyn George of Palo Alto Stanford (PAST) Heritage, April Halberstadt, Erin Herzog of the California History Room, Johanna Fassbender of the Los Altos History Museum, Allan Greenberg, Fred Holabird, Tom Howard of the Gilroy Museum, Leilani Marshall of the Sourisseau Academy, Vickie Mayer of the California Architects Board, Catherine Mills of History San José, Kim Moreno, Dori Myer of the Los Gatos History Room, Pam Navrat of the Harvey County (Kansas) Historical Society, Diana Petersen, Elizabeth Rhein, Anna Rosenbluth of the Ainsley House, Jeanine Stanek of the Sunnyvale Heritage Park Museum, Frank Van Rooy, and Beth Wyman.

Thank you also to Rebecca Kohn, Diane Malstrom, and Stephanie Watson of SJSU Special Collections & Archives. And a big thank you to Patrice Greene-Haggerty for accompanying me on many search-and-find missions.

I can't give enough thanks to photographer Sunny Scott, who has allowed me use of her beautiful photographs of the Gertrude Gardiner apartment building at Stanford and the Dudfield house in Palo Alto, and who took the author's photo used on the back cover of this book.

Lastly, thanks to a friend whose presence is deeply missed—the late Helen Stevens. She was looking forward to this book and I am sad that she wasn't able to see it come to fruition.

Krista Van Laan
January, 2017

What's in a Wolfe & Higgins Home?

Wolfe & Higgins used favorite features repeatedly, always in different combinations to give each residence a unique look. Here is a guideline to help you recognize a Wolfe & Higgins house.

House styles:

- Spanish Revival of one or two stories, almost always with a tiled roof. Typically, the house has a combination of a flat roof and shed, hipped, and/ or gabled roof, often with a centered flat roof and stepped levels of sloped roofs.

- Tudor Revival with multiple front gables and multi-level eaves, or with a jerkinhead (clipped) roof

- Italian Renaissance Revival with hipped roof and exposed rafters

- Dutch Colonial Revival with gambrel roof

Porch and entrance features:

- Arcaded off-center porch

- Elaborate front porch with pediment and many pillars

- Churrigueresque door surround

- Semicircular steps

Groups of three:

Windows, doors, arches, pillars, and decorative elements are frequently presented in triple sets

Windows and doors:

- The arch is the pervasive form, appearing in doors, windows, wing walls, porches, ornamentation, and insets. The most common formation

ABOVE: The basic styles of Wolfe & Higgins: Spanish Revival two-story and one-story, Tudor Revival, Italian Renaissance Revival, and Dutch Colonial Revival.

RIGHT, FROM TOP: Jerkinhead roof, pedimented porch with pillars, arcaded porch, semicircular porch with railed balcony and circular steps, Churrigueresque door surround.

is three arched windows separated by Tuscan columns or twisted spiral (also called barley sugar or Solomonic) columns.

- Large arched focal window with divided panes.

- Small arched window, usually with wrought-iron balcony, centered above the main entrance or focal window

Pillars and pilasters:

- Twisted spiral columns or pilasters. They are almost always between the windows or the window panes, sometimes appearing as accents to frame an entry or window.

- Columns with Tuscan, Ionic, or Corinthian capitals

Balconies

- Wrought iron, or with turned balusters

- Radius balconies with fluted bowls

Decorative elements:

- Sculpted plasterwork, terracotta, or stucco in the form of cartouches (oval or oblong element edged with ornamental scrollwork), escutcheons (shields), rosettes, and scallops

- Wrought-iron grilles and railings

- Balusters and bead-and-reel and other turned moldings

- False shutters with cutouts

- Corbels and brackets decorated with scrollwork

- Decorative chimneys

THIS PAGE: Some of the architectural elements typically seen on a Wolfe & Higgins building, including arched doors, windows, and porches; balconies; Tuscan columns and twisted spiral columns; wrought iron; and a number of different decorative elements.

Introduction

Frank Delos Wolfe and William Ernest Higgins formed their architectural partnership in November of 1917. Higgins, who had been working from his home in the city of Santa Clara, moved into Wolfe's office in the Auzerais Building on Santa Clara Street in downtown San José.

Frank Wolfe had always been a leader in residential design in the Santa Clara Valley. When his partnership with William Higgins began, Wolfe was already a well-known master architect with nearly thirty years of experience and about 700 projects to his credit. However, the types of architecture Frank Wolfe had produced over the previous decade—Mission Revival, Craftsman, and predominantly, Prairie—were starting to lose favor by the end of the 1910s. Wolfe had gained local and national recognition for his Prairie School architecture inspired by Frank Lloyd Wright, but that style, wildly popular when he introduced it in 1912, had run its course by the onset of World War I.

THIS PAGE AND OPPOSITE PAGE: Some examples of Wolfe & Higgins Spanish Revival residential design.

William Higgins was less established. Although he had been granted his architectural license in 1913, it was only very recently that his reputation and career had begun to take off, thanks to impressive jobs done for prominent local clients. In 1917, Higgins's reputation was such that he was hired by developer Francis Costello to design sixty unique homes for a new Los Altos development called Costello Acres. By July, Higgins had completed plans for ten of the houses, and it is very likely that this lucrative commission was his contribution to the new partnership and was worked on through 1918. Costello Acres still exists today, but in this very upscale neighborhood with its one-acre lots, the original houses have been demolished and replaced with much bigger ones.

A partnership was probably a wise choice for the architects. In April of 1917, the United States had entered into World War I and building in Santa Clara County had definitely slowed down. Pooling their resources could help the architects during this uncertain time.

It wasn't until 1919, when postwar building began, that business really took off for the partners. They went on to produce a prodigious amount of work, finishing over 500 completed projects by the firm's end in 1931.

The firm had many areas of proficiency. The architects worked on at least twenty-five school projects during the fourteen years they were in business together, some of them schools widely known for their beauty and modern design. More than twenty percent of their business involved designing commercial and nonresidential buildings, including stores, churches, canneries, creameries, and public buildings. They also specialized in apartment buildings and other types of multiple-unit dwellings such as duplexes and triplexes, using innovative design techniques for this type of housing that was still rather new.

Primarily, however, the firm of Wolfe & Higgins was known for single-family residential design. The rise in suburban living in the affluent 1920s and the architects' ability to home in on the tastes of their clientele was reflected in the ever-increasing amount of business at the firm of Wolfe & Higgins.

During its fourteen years of existence, Wolfe & Higgins worked in a limited number of styles. Dutch Colonial Revival (a favorite of William Higgins), Tudor Revival (a favorite of Carl Wolfe), and Italian Renaissance Revival were part of their portfolio. However, the style at which they excelled, and that appealed to homeowners of all economic levels, was Spanish Revival (often called, and perhaps more accurately labeled, Spanish Eclectic, due to the free mixture of different Spanish and Mediterranean stylistic elements). It was this that was to become the signature style of Wolfe & Higgins.

Throughout his entire career, Frank Wolfe was responsive to the needs of the Northern Californian homeowner, always slightly ahead of the trends in residential design. The firm's use of the Spanish Revival style during the 1920s, a style that appealed to so many homeowners, cemented the architects' position as top residential designers in their area. Although other architects in the

Santa Clara Valley also worked in the Spanish Revival style, few began so early and no one else matched the output of Wolfe & Higgins during this time. For homeowners who wanted a two- or three-bedroom bungalow, a Wolfe & Higgins Spanish Revival design provided a distinctive, unique, and beautiful yet affordable home with a roomy layout. For a wealthy customer such as attorney Robert Wright or political boss Charles Bigley, the same style could be applied to an impressive residence that reflected their tastes and status.

But Spanish Revival wasn't just for residential design. The stylish Spanish Revival facade made its appearance on Wolfe & Higgins-designed commercial and public buildings. Automobile showrooms and repair service buildings, in particular, were often designed with ornate Spanish Revival features.

A romantic re-imagining of Spanish architecture, Spanish Revival borrows from the entire history of Spanish architecture. Wolfe & Higgins, like many of the architects who worked in this style, applied a wide range of types of features, not necessarily knowing, or caring, whether something was Andalusian or Mission Revival or Spanish Baroque as they blended features in a harmonious manner.

Typical features of the California 1920s-era Spanish Revival buildings were barrel- or S-shaped red tile roofs with little or no overhang on an

BELOW AND RIGHT: California Tower, Balboa Park, by Architect Bertram Goodhue for the Panama-California Exposition.

The still-standing California Building is an icon of San Diego. Today the building houses the San Diego Museum of Man.

asymmetrical stucco building with arched doors and windows, twisted spiral columns, turrets, and balconies. Ornamental features include decorative chimneys and window grilles, decorative tiles, wrought iron, and sculptural terracotta or plasterwork. Wolfe & Higgins tried them all. The architects were also influenced by the elaborate ornamentation known as Churrigueresque, a Spanish Baroque style of architecture named after the Spanish architect and sculptor José Benito de Churriguera, who worked in Madrid and Salamanca in the late 1600s.

The architects also had no hesitation about incorporating features not necessarily associated with the style, adding Prairie or Colonial Revival or Beaux Arts features as they chose. Wolfe had never been afraid to mix it up in his designs—if he liked something, he used it—and he continued to include favored elements that he had been using for over two decades, such as dentil and egg-and-dart molding, square Prairie-style pillars and low brick walls with contrasting caps, sculpted plasterwork, and enormous focal windows. Wolfe had years of experience designing Mission Revival buildings. Mission Revival, along with Mediterranean Revival, can be said to be one of the stylistic predecessors of the Spanish Revival style that gained such popularity in California in the 1920s. Mission Revival, inspired by the nineteenth-century Spanish missions of California, included architectural elements such as stucco or plaster siding with roof parapets, exposed rafters, and quatrefoil windows, features that became part of the Spanish Revival style.

Interest in Spanish Revival architecture stemmed from the San Diego Panama-California Exposition, held from 1915 to 1917 in San Diego

RIGHT: Casa del Prado, a historic reconstruction of the original building from the 1915 Panama-California Exposition, is one of the most recognizable buildings in Balboa Park. This is one of the structures that was intended to be temporary, but has since been rebuilt to be permanent.

BELOW LEFT: Arcaded walkway in Balboa Park.

BELOW RIGHT: The Hayes Mansion in San José was designed for Mary Chynoweth by architect George Page in 1903. Listed on the National Register of Historic Places, the Hayes Mansion is considered to be one of the best examples of Mediterranean Revival architecture in the Santa Clara Valley. Mediterranean Revival, along with Mission Revival, paved the way for the intense interest in Spanish Colonial Revival in California.

TOP: George Washington Smith's 1918 Santa Barbara house as shown in the *Architectural Forum*.

ABOVE: Architect Julia Morgan's masterpiece, Hearst Castle, is one of California's best-known examples of the Spanish Colonial Revival style.

to celebrate the opening of the Panama Canal. The Exposition was one of the only such events that ever featured a single style of architecture, called Spanish Colonial Revival, which was rooted in the architecture of the missions and the Spanish colonial legacy of the West. Bertram Grosvenor Goodhue, hired as the Exposition's chief architect, was also greatly influenced by time spent in Mexico when he was in his twenties. Goodhue's continuing love for Mexico, its landscape, people, and architecture, informed his designs.

Planned since 1909 by the San Diego Chamber of Commerce, the Exposition was held in City Park, renamed Balboa Park to honor Spanish-born Vasco de Balboa, the first European to spot the Pacific Ocean while on exploration in Panama. Some of the Exposition structures were intended to be used later as museums, galleries, and state buildings, but Goodhue expected most of them to be temporary. Despite the expectation that they would last only a year, many of them lasted into the 1960s, and today, a group called The Committee of One Hundred strives to rebuild the previously demolished buildings and preserve those that still exist.

Goodhue himself designed the buildings in the California Quadrangle, including the California Building and iconic California Tower, always intended to be permanent. These buildings featured the work of a family of master sculptors and stonecutters, the Piccirilli brothers of New York.

"Within these confines was built a city-in-miniature wherein everything that met the eye and ear of the visitor were meant to recall to mind the glamour and mystery and poetry of the old Spanish days," said Goodhue. Today, Goodhue's city-in-miniature is a National Historic Landmark District.

The style took hold of California, supplanting the domination of the Craftsman bungalow. Architect George Washington Smith of Santa Barbara applied the Spanish Revival style to his own home in 1918 and went on to do groundbreaking work in this style. Because of his work and that of James Osborne Craig and Mary McLaughlin Craig, the

ABOVE LEFT: Frank Wolfe had begun exploring Spanish Revival architecture before partnering with William Higgins. Above is his 1916 house designed for Dr. James and May Tebbetts of Hollister, perhaps his first use of the triple arches that appeared on nearly all of the Spanish Revival Wolfe & Higgins buildings after 1921.

ABOVE RIGHT: Also in 1916, Frank Wolfe designed this Mission Revival/ Spanish-style house with arched entrance for Dr. Frederick B. Pearce and his wife Edna of San José.

BELOW: Churrigueresque door surround on the Wolfe & Higgins Grace Spencer Hall home.

city of Santa Barbara adopted Spanish Colonial Revival as its official style when rebuilding after a 1925 earthquake. In Los Angeles, Wallace Neff and the firm of Morgan, Walls and Clements were among those who applied the Spanish Revival style to produce richly ornamented stores, theaters, houses, and commercial buildings for the golden age of Hollywood and its environs. In San Francisco, architects such as Julia Morgan and Weeks & Day worked in this style to design some of their greatest works.

Frank Wolfe and William Higgins were most certainly aware of the Panama Exposition and its subsequent influence on California architecture. Before the Exposition, the *San Jose Mercury Herald* ran several articles trumpeting the upcoming event, saying, in a 1911 article, "San Diego will hold the most beautiful, unique, and artistic exposition ever arranged...in beauty and extent." Many of the architectural trade magazines to which the architects subscribed heralded the plans of the Panama Exposition, including the April 1914 issue of *The Architectural Review,* which contained an article by architect Bertram Goodhue showing illustrations of and discussing the plans for the exposition's magnificent buildings.

Throughout the 1920s, architectural trade magazines such as *Architect and Engineer of California* and the *Pacific Coast Architect* published article after article focusing on Spanish Revival residential and commercial architecture in California. The style became available to consumers, as well; the 1923 *Pacific Ready-Cut Homes* catalog, for example, contained more than fifteen Spanish Revival kit houses plus duplexes, apartment buildings, and bungalow courts.

Wolfe & Higgins were early adopters of the Spanish Revival style in Northern California, and by 1922 were working almost exclusively in it. At the beginning of that year, they gained important local awareness of their Spanish Revival work with an outstanding residence for heiress Grace Spencer Hall. (See page 80.) The January 2, 1922 *San Jose Mercury Herald* contained a story with a large picture of the Hall house with its grand Churrigueresque entrance. "Truly Spanish," said both architect and client as they admired the house.

About
the
Architects

Frank Delos Wolfe
(1862-1926).

Frank Delos Wolfe

Architect Frank Delos Wolfe of San José, California, was one of the most prolific architects of his time. From 1888, when he moved to San José as a builder and would-be architect, until his death in 1926, he was responsible, both alone and with partners, for more than one thousand works in Northern California. Eight of his works are today on the National Register of Historic Places and a great number of them are designated landmarks of the cities in which they are located. Several of his designs have been the subjects of the national Historic American Buildings Survey (HABS) reports. The list of buildings attributed to Frank Wolfe still grows as research into his work continues.

The Early Years

Frank Delos Wolfe came from a long line of skilled carpenters and craftsmen. His paternal grandfather Andrew Wolfe was a carpenter, and his paternal grandmother Salome Gerber was the daughter and sister of carpenters. Andrew Wolfe retired from carpentry to a life of farming, and he and Salome settled in Sandusky County, Ohio, where they raised three sons and five daughters. Their youngest son, Jeremiah Bell Wolfe, the future father of Frank Delos Wolfe, was born in 1840.

Jeremiah married local farmer's daughter Susan Kelsey Dawley in 1861 and the couple moved to Ballville Township in Sandusky County, Ohio, where Jeremiah worked as a carpenter, and also did some farming. Their first child Frank Delos was born September 29, 1862, in Fremont. Shortly after Frank's birth, Jeremiah and his brother Daniel, along with more than 300,000 other young men in the state of Ohio, joined the Union army to fight in the Civil War. When Jeremiah returned, he and Susan had three more children: Cora, Ernest Linwood, and Edith Belle.

Most of the men in the Wolfe clan were carpenters, many of them renowned for their skills. Both Frank Wolfe and his brother Ernest Linwood (later known as "E.L.") learned carpentry at home, well enough so they were later able to make a living from it. Frank, however, unlike his father and brother and cousins, had aspirations to be an architect. In those days, it was possible to become an architect without obtaining a related university degree and a license, but it was still not easy. Frank Wolfe was to spend his early adult life working to achieve this goal.

TOP: Nellie Crockett Wolfe (1867-1962).

ABOVE: Jeremiah Bell Wolfe (1840-1919) and E.L. Wolfe (1870-1953).

RIGHT: Drawing of the Bretch building. It is likely that this drawing is by Frank Wolfe, as he was working for Ross when this building was designed.

BELOW: Carl Jay Wolfe (1888-1931).

When he was twenty-four years old, Wolfe married Ellen "Nellie" Crockett, a well-educated young woman from nearby Green Springs, Ohio. Five years his junior and a graduate of the prestigious Green Springs Academy, she was the fourth of ten children of teacher Edward Crockett and his wife Eliza.

Right after their marriage, the couple moved to Newton, Kansas, where Wolfe had found employment with architect William L. Ross. Newton, the county seat of Harvey County, was a new and growing city when the Wolfes arrived. In the late 1870s through the 1880s, it experienced a building boom and attracted builders and architects. William L. Ross had moved there from La Harpe, Illinois in the late 1880s to take advantage of the boom and immediately had his hands full with commercial and residential projects, the largest being a three-story building funded by the Bretch grocery firm to be leased to the county for use as a courthouse. (In 1906, a new courthouse was built and the Bretch brothers took back their building to use for their wholesale and retail grocery business.) Frank Wolfe probably worked as a draftsman for Ross, gaining invaluable training in his quest to become a professional architect.

The Wolfes' first child, son Carl, was born in Newton on January 16, 1888. That same year, the Wolfes moved to San José, California, joined by Frank's parents, Jeremiah and Susan, and his three siblings. San José, with its rich orchard land and ideal weather, was undergoing its own building boom, one that would continue for many years.

Frank, his father Jeremiah, and his brother E.L. all found work right away as builders. By the following year, Jeremiah and Frank had begun to buy land. In September of 1889, Frank Wolfe built a house on Seventh Street in San José, a "cottage" at a cost of $1,879. This was the first of many spec houses Wolfe designed and built in San José.

Frank and Nellie Wolfe had their second child, daughter Edith Blanche (1889-1966), and the family settled into life in San José, working hard to become prosperous and further Wolfe's career. The family moved from

TOP: Judge Gass's 1891 house as it looks today.

ABOVE: One of Frank Wolfe's many homes in San José.

RIGHT: The King Conservatory of Music was Frank Wolfe's first major commission.

one house to another as Frank Wolfe designed and built houses to showcase his skills. Nellie would work on the landscaping and interior decor and they would either live in the house for a short time or sell it and move on. They moved frequently in their early years in San José, living in at least twelve different places between 1888 and 1907, after which, probably due to Wolfe's financial success, they stayed in their homes for longer periods of time.

In the early 1890s, Wolfe was the contractor, and almost certainly the designer, on a number of houses in San José, including an 1891 house for prominent justice of the peace John William Gass. In 1892, Wolfe received a major break when he was hired to design the San José King Conservatory of Music for impresario Frank "Loui" King. The Conservatory's sizable catalog included a picture of the buildings and cited Wolfe as the architect. Wolfe started listing himself as an architect in the city directory and got additional work in other cities such as Palo Alto and Sunnyvale. He began to join fraternal organizations including the Elks and Odd Fellows, which became the source of most of his jobs.

In the 1890s, Wolfe had competition from many established architects in San José. The newspapers regularly published articles detailing the architects' work, a sign of the city's progress and prosperity. As an article from the *San Jose Evening News* in 1892 stated:

> Undoubtedly building operations are as extensive and progressing as rapidly in San Jose at present as at any time in its history. Over sixty buildings of all kinds are now in course of construction. The value of these improvements when completed will be over $600,000. An encouraging feature of the building operation is the large number of fine residences that are being erected at a cost of from $3000 to $12,000 each.

The article went on to list the work in progress and the architects responsible: Theodore Lenzen and Jacob Lenzen & Sons, William D. Van Sicklen, George W. Page, Francis Reid. These men, along with Joseph O. McKee and William Klinkert were responsible for most of the architect-designed buildings in San José.

No one did more work at that time than the two firms headed by the Lenzen brothers. Theodore Lenzen and his brother Jacob, along with their architect sons, had designed or would design most of the significant buildings in the city. The Lenzens advertised heavily (although their reputation was such that they may not have had to), with large display ads, and multiple ads in the city directories and newspapers and tourist books.

Frank Wolfe followed their lead and took out his own ad in the Classified Business section of the 1892 San José city directory. He listed himself under Architects, and went to the added expense of putting his name in bold block letters.

The Wolfe & McKenzie Years

In 1894, architect Joseph O. McKee retired, and by 1896, Frank Wolfe had acquired McKee's business and his employee, draftsman Charles S. McKenzie. McKenzie was just over twenty years old at the time of the acquisition.

Charles McKenzie lived in downtown San José with his two older sisters and widowed mother Jane. His father had died when Charles was a young child and the whole family worked to support the household, mother Jane and sister Maude as dressmakers, and sister Lillie as a teacher. Charles left school at the age of fourteen to work, finding a job with architect McKee when he was eighteen. While Charles did not have an educational background or family connections, his artistic talents (McKenzie was to later become known as a skilled fine-arts painter) may have made him especially suitable for the job.

McKenzie was a talented enough draftsman that Wolfe kept him on after taking over the business, and by 1900, made him a partner. The pair moved into the newly built Smout Building in downtown San José, acquired a new draftsman, and, due to an ever-increasing building boom, soon became one of the busiest architectural offices in the area. Charles McKenzie's mother and sisters were able to move from a rental to their own home, fully paid for, and Charles married Edwina Birchler in 1903.

Wolfe & McKenzie were tremendously prolific, responsible for hundreds of projects during their eleven years together, including four that are today on the National Register of Historic Places. The pair was successful working in popular styles such as Mission Revival and Craftsman. Their Mission Revival work included the 1903 San José Sperry Flour Building (a San José City Landmark today), the San José Fire Station, and houses and apartment buildings. Their Craftsman designs included several houses on Martin Avenue in the Hanchett Residence Park in San José, an

ABOVE: Charles McKenzie (1874-1957).

BELOW: Wolfe & McKenzie's 1903 Mission Revival Sperry Flour Company, still standing today, is a San José City Landmark.

BOTTOM: The 1907 San José Fire Station, since demolished, was another example of Wolfe & McKenzie's Mission Revival work.

ABOVE LEFT: Wolfe & McKenzie designed this house in 1905 for Lucie and John Chace of San José.

ABOVE RIGHT: This 1905 house was designed in San José for Herbert E. Cox, president of the Pacific Coast Business College.

BELOW: The Hanchett Residence Park Wolfe & McKenzie Craftsman homes, one of which is shown below, were considered to be significant examples of the style by the Historic American Buildings Survey.

upscale neighborhood developed in 1907 by Lewis Hanchett on the site of the Agricultural Park amusement and exhibition grounds. These iconic Craftsman homes were documented in a Historic American Buildings Survey (HABS) report in 1979.

Wolfe & McKenzie's most distinctive work must be the houses that reflected their own eclectic style. Frank Wolfe and Charles McKenzie together had a gift for residential design—and the growing population had money to spend and wanted homes that were modern, distinctive, and "artistic," one of the highest compliments that could be given to a house at the turn of the twentieth century in the Santa Clara Valley. As George Espinola wrote in *Cottages, Flats, Buildings and Bungalows*:

> Wolfe & McKenzie's floor plans were perfectly suited for the emerging middle class of their time. The doctors, lawyers, bankers, realtors, and insurance agents that made up their clientele wanted no-nonsense floor plans that were efficient and functional, combined with artistically designed exteriors that demonstrated to their neighbors that they had taste.

Wolfe & McKenzie mixed elements together in ways that resulted in houses that were practical and elegant and very often unusual. Quatrefoil windows, a favorite, could appear not only as expected on a Mission Revival building, but also on a Dutch Colonial-style home with a gambrel roof. Craftsman-like exposed roof rafters might be incorporated into a house that had Victorian features.

There are several characteristics that can be said to define the Wolfe & McKenzie style. The roof is often hipped with a central dormer and deep

TOP: The Alviso Yacht Club, designed by Wolfe & McKenzie, is still in use today.

ABOVE CENTER: Wolfe & McKenzie worked together on only one project after their 1910 split: a new Elks Lodge that was a design collaboration between architects Frank Wolfe, Louis Lenzen, Charles McKenzie, and William Binder, all of whom were Elks members.

ABOVE: Charles McKenzie continued to excel in residential design in San José. This is the last house in which he lived with his wife Edwina.

overhangs, sometimes boxed, sometimes with exposed rafters. Upper stories are complex, sometimes cantilevered or with cantilevered elements such as projecting corner windows, balconies, or towers. Porches were usually wide, with Tuscan or Corinthian columns, and there was typically a balcony, either decorative or functional. Rooms often had curved walls and half-circle bow windows, sometimes breaking out of the corners of the structure. Objects—gables, dormers, chimneys, or smaller roofs—often broke up through the roof as well.

In 1902, developer T.S. Montgomery opened a new 120-acre residential tract called Naglee Park in San José, and it is here that the wide range of Wolfe & McKenzie's residential work can still be seen today. Naglee Park was built from the vast grounds of the estate of Civil War general Henry Morris Naglee. Advertised as being a "first-class residence neighborhood in every respect," with "not an objectionable feature," the tract had large lots and strict building codes. Stores, wood yards, and places of business were forbidden, with barns restricted to suitable distances from the street. In April of 1902, work began laying the streets, and lots sold rapidly.

All of the top local architects—and some, including master Berkeley architect Bernard Maybeck, from farther afield—were called upon to design homes for this new subdivision, resulting in a mixture of the finest and newest residential design in the area, and a neighborhood that retains its beauty more than a century later. Wolfe & McKenzie, during their years together and subsequent years apart, were responsible for more Naglee Park home designs than were any other architects.

Wolfe & McKenzie's output was prodigious, and not limited to San José. The firm did work for clients in Mountain View, Napa, Pacific Grove, Hollister, Palo Alto, and cities all over Northern California. Nor did they only design residences. Some of their most significant works were schools, commercial, and public buildings.

In 1903, J.O. McKee, who in his retirement was pursuing his greatest love, sailing, hired Wolfe & McKenzie to design the new clubhouse for the South Bay Yacht Club in Alviso, which McKee had helped to found in 1888. That building, one of the oldest yacht clubs in Northern California, is still standing and in use as a yacht club today.

In 1905, Wolfe & McKenzie designed the city hall in Gilroy, today the symbol of Gilroy and on the National Register of Historic Places. The distinctive building might be described as Mission Revival, but with its turrets and gingerbread and Arabesque windows, has been called "Flemish Baroque" by admiring locals.

ABOVE: Wolfe & McKenzie designed the 1905 Gilroy City Hall, today on the National Register of Historic Places, and a symbol of the town of Gilroy.

In 1907, Wolfe & McKenzie published a catalog of their work called the *Book of Designs*. This book contained photographs, cost estimates, and plans of ninety-six of their residential designs, many of which are still standing today. This gave their business a great boost, resulting in more than eighty projects the following year.

At the end of 1910, Wolfe & McKenzie dissolved their partnership. The reasons are not known; it is probable that Charles McKenzie initiated the separation to give himself independence. McKenzie went on to run a very successful single proprietorship. He stayed in business until 1942 and donated his time to the military after retiring. He was responsible for many notable buildings in San José, both residential and commercial. McKenzie died in Santa Clara, California, January 9, 1957 at the age of eighty-two.

The Sole Proprietorship Years

In 1911, Frank Wolfe was on his own. He was up against competition from not only the newly acclaimed local architects such as William Binder and Warren Skillings, but he had to compete against his former partner, Charles McKenzie, for the same types of jobs. He was one of the best-known architects in San José, however, and he found work. He also continued to buy land and design spec houses that his brother E.L. Wolfe would build.

Wolfe produced some of his best work the first year he was on his own. He designed a number of notable buildings in the Mission Revival style, including residences for Palo Alto stock trader Reese Evans and his wife Annie, Santa Clara banking mogul and real estate developer Robert Fatjo and his wife Teresa, and a block of stores in Campbell for developer B.O. Curry.

In Hayward, Wolfe designed an eighteen-room residence for Emil and Ada Burr. This house, a transitional work between his residential designs

TOP: 1911 Mission Revival house for Reese Evans in Palo Alto (demolished).

ABOVE CENTER: 1911 Craftsman house for Gertrude Huff of Palo Alto.

ABOVE: The 1911 Burr house in Hayward. Originally intended to be nine rooms, it had eighteen rooms by the time it was completed.

of the McKenzie years and the Prairie buildings that came after, features cantilevered corner windows like a Wolfe & McKenzie house, and exposed rafter tails, square piers, and horizontal lines like a Wolfe Prairie house.

Wolfe also produced a number of Craftsman houses during this period. In 1911, Gertrude Huff of Palo Alto commissioned a Craftsman home, as did Charles Miller (whose Saratoga Craftsman house is today on the National Register of Historic Places). Orchardist Paul Cordes of Gilroy commissioned a magnificent Craftsman house in 1912.

In 1912, Frank Wolfe introduced something completely new: a house inspired by the famous

RIGHT: This Mission Revival house was designed in 1911 for the Fatjo family of Santa Clara.

Midwestern architect Frank Lloyd Wright. This asymmetrical house designed in the Prairie style was built in the North Willow Glen section of San José, and was Frank and Nellie Wolfe's personal residence. The style was immediately in great demand. Within the year, Wolfe designed six more of these houses for influential locals, one of them a commanding residence for Peter and Blanche Col, which has become one of Wolfe's best-known works. Wolfe's son Carl joined the firm as an associate and the firm became known as Wolfe & Wolfe. Prairie became their signature style.

Prairie was a school of architecture that originated in Chicago in the 1890s, started by a group of young architects who wanted to create a style

ABOVE LEFT: The Miller-Melone house in Saratoga is on the National Register of Historic Places.

LEFT: Paul Cordes's Craftsman house in Gilroy.

RIGHT: The first of Frank Wolfe's Prairie-style homes was this 1912 house he designed for himself and his wife Nellie. The Wolfes kept this house for nine years.

ABOVE: In 1916, Frank Wolfe and local master architect Theodore Lenzen offered their services pro bono to design this log cabin for the Vendome Parlor of the Native Daughters, who erected it as a memorial to the pioneers. The cabin still stands today in Alum Rock Park and is a San José City Landmark.

Courtesy, History San José.

ABOVE: Pendent tiles such as those shown above were a signature feature of Wolfe during his Prairie era.

that was uniquely American. Frank Lloyd Wright was the most famous of the Prairie architects, but by no means the only one.

The Prairie style was identified with the Midwest, where wide-open land could accommodate this type of building with its large footprint. Prairie architecture's defining characteristic is an emphasis on horizontal orientation and cubic massing—that is, the building is made up of cubic forms that emphasize the horizontal lines. The buildings have low-pitched or flat roofs with deep overhanging boxed eaves. Windows are set in horizontal bands, often with geometric stained glass patterns, and there is typically a horizontal band of clerestory windows (windows above eye level). Rooms are wide open and traffic flows through these houses, as opposed to Victorian or even Craftsman homes with their small, enclosed rooms. The buildings were intended to harmonize with nature and blend in with the landscape, both in form and materials.

The Prairie school of architecture was almost unknown in California. In 1909, Frank Lloyd Wright had designed one Prairie-style house in California—the George Stewart house in Montecito—and notable Prairie architect Walter Burley Griffin designed a house for John Dickinson in Hollister (today on the grounds of the Pietra Santa Winery). But there was not much else, and in San José, these buildings were brand new.

Frank Wolfe freely drew from Frank Lloyd Wright, but he made the style his own in a way that suited his California clientele. The Prairie-style houses he designed were one or two stories, with flat or low-pitched hipped roofs with deep overhangs. The eaves were boxed, and Wolfe added decorative friezes in classical designs. The main room was typically one and one-half stories with clerestory windows with stained glass Frank Lloyd Wright-inspired designs. All of the Wolfe Prairies have a large plate glass picture window in the living room, some of them as big as twelve feet wide. Wolfe liked ornamentation: his signature feature was a set of pendent decorative tiles that were embedded into the stucco at the end of vertical wooden strips, made to look as if they were hanging from ribbons from below the eave. Wolfe's Prairie buildings also often incorporated ornate plasterwork inspired by Chicago architect and Frank Lloyd Wright mentor Louis Sullivan, along with moldings of classical designs such as those Wolfe had worked with since his pre-McKenzie days: egg-and-dart, frets, and dentil patterns.

Wolfe & Wolfe applied the Prairie style to houses, apartment buildings, and a number of schools. Their use of this style helped gain the firm national attention in *The Western Architect*, which featured many

ABOVE: One of Wolfe's first Frank Lloyd Wright-influenced Prairie-style buildings was this 1912 house designed for Blanche and Peter Col. The Col house may be the best-known of all of Frank Wolfe's works. In 1979, it was the subject of a Historic American Buildings Survey (HABS) report.

RIGHT: A 1914 Modern house for Cora and Fremont Older at Woodhills, their Cupertino ranch. The house, today on the National Register of Historic Places, was also the subject of a HABS report in 1977.

BELOW: 1913 Moorish mansion for A. Kingsley and Myrtle Macomber at Paicines Ranch near Hollister.

Wolfe & Wolfe works in 1914. The architects were also featured extensively in the west coast's architectural trade magazine, *The Architect and Engineer of California*, which had published photographs of Wolfe's work since the early Wolfe & McKenzie years. In February 1914, the firm of Wolfe & Wolfe was the subject of a sixteen-page article in *The Architect and Engineer* that focused on their "different" architecture, stating, "...a few houses they have designed are so unusual in their treatment that the critics are bound to be heard from."

Although Wolfe was best known for Prairie-style architecture in the years from 1912 to 1918, he produced many other outstanding works, some of them reinforcing the claim to "different" architecture. In 1913, he designed a Moorish mansion outside of Hollister for A. Kingsley Macomber, a wealthy racehorse and cattle breeder and husband of Myrtle Harkness, heiress to the Standard Oil fortune. In 1914, Wolfe designed a Modern (in every sense of the word) house in Cupertino for social reformers Fremont and Cora Older. Fremont Older was editor of the major newspapers in San Francisco and Cora was a writer and preservationist. Their house was a flat-roofed two-story house with no eaves and little decoration. In 1915, Wolfe designed a residence in Tres Pinos for socialite Julia Bolado Davis and her husband Frank. The house,

ABOVE: "Casa Grande," designed for Frank and Julia Bolado Davis of Tres Pinos is one of Wolfe's most outstanding Mission Revival residential designs.

BELOW RIGHT: The 1916 Prairie house for San José attorney Charles Allen and his wife Carrie shows the Frank Lloyd Wright influence.

aptly named "Casa Grande," is one of Wolfe's best Mission Revival works. During these years, Wolfe continued to channel Frank Lloyd Wright, with buildings such as a two-story Prairie house designed for attorney Charles Allen.

By 1917, tastes started to change and the Prairie style was no longer so popular. (It almost completely disappeared from Wolfe's repertoire only a few years later.) The United States entered World War I and building was greatly curtailed. Things changed on a personal level for Frank Wolfe as well. His beloved mother Susan died at age seventy-six. His son Carl enlisted in the Marines in June of 1917. And it appears that his health may have begun to decline. At the end of 1917, Wolfe decided to go into business with architect William Ernest Higgins.

William Ernest Higgins

William Ernest Higgins
(1871–1936).

It was not until around 1916, when he was in his mid-thirties, that William Higgins of Santa Clara, California, gained recognition as a local architect, just about a year before he became a partner in Frank Wolfe's business. Today, only a few buildings are identified as having been designed by Higgins before he partnered with Wolfe.

The family tree of William Higgins holds a cast of colorful characters—pioneers, entrepreneurs, and artists. His maternal grandmother Louisa Harlow came from an early American New England family, some of whose members were born on the Mayflower or in Plymouth Colony; others fought in the Revolutionary War. When Louisa Harlow's mother died, the family moved from Maine to Illinois where Louisa met and married William Smith. In 1846, their daughter Lucinda Emma (Lucy), the future mother of William Ernest Higgins, was born.

In 1850, William and Louisa Smith and baby Lucy left Illinois for California in a wagon drawn by a team of oxen, an arduous trip that took several years. The party stopped in Missouri, where Louisa gave birth to their second child, a son, William Gustavus, before continuing on their way. They made it to Santa Clara, California in 1853.

According to family lore, when the Smiths arrived in Santa Clara, they traded their covered wagon and team for a two-room house. William Smith found work as a brick mason and later as a stock-raiser, and the family slowly became more prosperous. Sometime around 1863, daughter Lucy met and married Rufus Higgins, a young man who had arrived not long before from Maine.

Rufus Leopold Higgins had grown up in the sawmill town of Sidney, Maine under what appear to have been difficult circumstances. His mother Sarah was divorced in 1849 with three young boys. In 1850, she was living in the household of Elias Bowman, a well-off farmer more than twenty years her senior, whom she later married. For unknown reasons, her sons were not able to stay at the Bowman home. The 1850 census shows a seven-year-old Rufus residing at a nearby farm; later, his brother Alpheus was sent to live on another family's farm. By 1860, Rufus,

RIGHT: This picture is believed to be of the two-room house that William and Louisa Smith acquired in 1853 when they arrived in Santa Clara.

only sixteen years old, had somehow made his way across the country to Santa Clara, where he found lodging with a local family and work as a day laborer.

Rufus apparently had considerable charm, for he and Lucy Smith were married sometime around 1863, when he was nineteen and she sixteen. Immediately following their marriage, they moved to Virginia City, Nevada, where they opened a store.

ABOVE LEFT AND RIGHT: Lucy (1846-1922) and Rufus Higgins (1844-1905). Lucy has gained some historical fame as a suffragist and close friend of Sarah Brown, daughter of the notorious abolitionist, John Brown, who led an 1859 revolt at Harper's Ferry, for which he was hanged.

John Brown's widow, Mary Ann Day Brown, moved to Saratoga in 1881 with daughters Sarah and Ellen. Rufus handled the sale of Brown's house and Lucy became friends with her daughter Sarah. The story of the friendship of Sarah Brown and Lucy Higgins was the subject of an episode of PBS's *History Detectives* in 2003.

Virginia City was founded in 1859 when Henry Tompkins Paige Comstock and others laid claim to land in western Nevada that would yield an enormous amount of silver and gold. The rush that ensued and lasted more than twenty years caused western Nevada to become a center of mining activity, with Virginia City its main hub. When Rufus and Lucy moved there in the early 1860s, Virginia City had recently gone from a town of tents and dugouts to a tremendously prosperous city with a population that reached 25,000 in the mid-1870s. (Today, its population is less than 900.) The city, 6,200 feet up a winding rocky mountain road in the Virginia Mountains, had mansions, many churches, a red-light district, luxury hotels, its own opera house, a state-of-the-art school, and stores that imported everything to cater to clients who spent vast amounts of money.

Rufus tried to make his fortune both through mining and as a merchant; he bought a soda mine and launched the Nevada Soda Mining Company, and also owned and ran a series of general stores in both Virginia City and nearby Reno. Lucy probably helped with the store; during this time, she also gained local recognition as a singer, performing at least once in the local opera house. The young couple became key figures in local society and their church, where Rufus, along with the governor of Nevada, was a trustee. By 1870, the couple's real estate was estimated at a rather astonishing value of $27,000. In 1871, their son William Ernest was born.

The Higginses' stores included a wide variety of stock. Advertisements in the Carson City, Nevada *Daily State Register* listed pianos, organs, musical instruments, sheet music (surely due to the influence of the musical Lucy), toys, and a "large assortment of FANCY GOODS..."

In the mid-1870s, Rufus launched a creative, and unusual, endeavor: he developed ink and sold it in his own custom-made bottles, embossed with the words "R.L. Higgins Virginia City." Those bottles, which today are some of the most valuable collectibles of their type, are among the only embossed ink bottles produced in the Western United States at that time.

ABOVE: The R.L. Higgins personalized ink bottles are among the rarest, and most valuable, of collectibles. In the early 2000s, one of Rufus Higgins's bottles sold for nearly $20,000.

It is believed that Higgins had these bottles manufactured in San Francisco around 1875, during a period in which Virginia City, and his store, were flourishing. Before he was able to fully launch his ink business, a fire destroyed Virginia City and the Higginses were unable to recover.

The rare Higgins ink bottles have been the subject of much speculation; mainly, was Rufus Higgins related to Charles M. Higgins, Ireland-born founder of the Brooklyn-based Higgins Ink Company, still in business today? And did Rufus's formula somehow wind up in the hands of Charles Higgins, who formed his company in 1880, right after Rufus and Lucy went bankrupt? While research shows that it is unlikely that there is a connection between Rufus of Maine and Charles of Brooklyn, the fact remains that Rufus and Lucy's whereabouts between 1876 and 1880 are not known, nor are the family trees of both Higgins families fully documented. These questions may always remain unanswered.

The Higginses did not have time to turn this new business into a success. In October of 1875, fire ravaged Virginia City. The city had been conserving water by turning it off at night, and firefighters were unable to do much as the fire moved through the city's wooden buildings. Tens of thousands were left homeless.

Within two years of the fire, Virginia City was rebuilt, but by then it was too late for Rufus and Lucy, who had lost everything. They filed for bankruptcy and in 1876, after thirteen years in Nevada, left Virginia City and returned to California.

Rufus soon was back on his feet. He became a real estate broker and founded the Santa Clara Valley Land and Loan Agency with offices in Santa Clara and San José; later, he went into the lumber business. The family lived with Lucy's mother Louisa and soon became part of Santa Clara society. Besides William Ernest, the Higginses had a son Alpheus (who was born in 1874 and died at the young age of six) and in 1887, their daughter Louise was born.

Lucy flourished in Santa Clara. She was a well-known singer who performed frequently at society and club events; she was also an illustrator and writer of short stories that she shared with her family. She was active in music circles, and in 1886, was part of the executive committee that raised money to build the Conservatory of Music at the College of the Pacific. She was a leader in the Santa Clara Woman's Club and other community organizations, and she and her mother Louisa both became involved in the suffrage movement.

California women were able to vote almost ten years before the 19th Amendment passed in 1920. Santa Clara County was the only Bay Area county to vote in support of women's suffrage in the October 10, 1911 election, thanks to the efforts of organizations such as the Woman's Club.

Less than two weeks before the election, Lucy Higgins presented a Suffrage Day with an Open Air Meeting in Santa Clara. The main speaker was Agnes Howe of the San Jose Normal School (now known as San José State University), president of the Central California Teachers' Association and a regular speaker at suffrage events. Rallies, meetings, and speakers continued in Santa Clara until the election.

This is the family in which William Ernest Higgins was brought up. The young William did not set out to be an architect. Like his mother, he was a lover of music; he was a professional-level flute-player who later helped form a symphony orchestra in San José in which he played, and he

ABOVE LEFT: The Higgins family home in Santa Clara.

ABOVE RIGHT: One of William Higgins's first architectural projects was to turn the Gothic Revival family home into a more fashionable and stripped-down Colonial Revival house.

BELOW: Rufus Higgins's stationery, used when he launched his new business in Santa Clara.

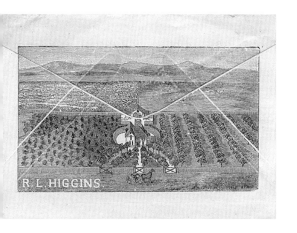

considered a career in the performing arts. In 1892, at the age of twenty-one, he worked for his father as the secretary of Rufus's North Coast Lumber Company until it went out of business in 1896, then worked as a clerk at the Quartermaster's Depot in San Francisco and later as secretary of the Western Land Company. In 1895, Higgins married Minnie Livingston of Santa Clara and their daughter Cornelia was born the following year. The marriage did not last long; the couple divorced less than ten years after they married. (In 1909, Higgins married twenty-two-year-old Anna Sophia Lewis, with whom he later had three children—Constance, William Lewis, and Barbara.)

Williams Higgins's father Rufus died in 1905 in a shocking accident. Rufus was ill and had been taking two types of medication—one a benign extract to be taken as a spoonful three times a day and the other the deadly poison aconite (aconitum), to be taken as a minute drop diluted in water. Rufus mistakenly reversed the medications; he took a full spoonful of the aconite and died within hours.

Higgins and his daughter Cornelia moved back to Santa Clara to live with the bereaved Lucy. Around this time, Higgins appears to have decided to become an architect, perhaps—like many architects—having gained experience designing homes while working in the lumber and land development business, or perhaps as a result of living with his mother and trying to decide what to do as a divorced man with a young daughter. Lucy Higgins was able to help her son achieve this goal.

Higgins advertised his services as an architect from 1907 to 1909, but no records exist today of any architectural work he may have done during that period or what training he received. In 1910, he worked as a draftsman in the office of the renowned San José architect William Binder. The

RIGHT: Higgins was hired to renovate the Santa Clara Woman's Club adobe building in 1914. Today, the historic adobe is a Registered California State Landmark.

experience with Binder apparently gave Higgins the training he needed. In May of 1913, he underwent an oral examination from the California State Board of Architecture and obtained his license.

Through her work at the Santa Clara Woman's Club, University of the Pacific, and other organizations, Lucy Higgins had connections throughout the county. In 1914, William Higgins landed what was perhaps his first big break, a commission for a major renovation on the Santa Clara Woman's Club. The Woman's Club, with Lucy Higgins as vice-president, had purchased and restored the last of the historic adobe buildings of the Second Mission of Santa Clara to save it from being demolished, and they were going to use it as a clubhouse, museum, and meeting place for the Historical Society.

As a significant show of faith, Lucy allowed Higgins to conduct a major renovation of the family house. The house, which had originally been the two-room cabin traded for a wagon and team of oxen, had grown over the years to a large Gothic Revival with many additions. Higgins stripped the gingerbread and removed the big front porch with its elaborate Gothic arches and turned it into a sleek side-gabled Colonial Revival with a shallow entry framed by two pilasters supporting a pediment above an arched door.

These beginnings led to other commissions for prominent local families. Few of the Higgins-designed buildings are still standing today. The still-extant residences designed by Higgins in 1916 and 1917 introduce many of the features that were to become important elements in the Wolfe & Higgins portfolio: ornate pillared porches, arched doors and windows, and grand entrance halls with spiraling staircase railings.

ABOVE: William Higgins designed this Dutch Colonial Revival house for Wilmer and Dorothy Gross in San José in 1916.

Dorothy and Wilmer Gross House
San José City Landmark

One of William Higgins's first commissions was a house on The Alameda in San José for Wilmer Gross and his fiancé Dorothy Davy. The Alameda, an important transportation corridor since the late 1700s, is a segment of El Camino Real, the 600-mile road that connected the California missions from San Diego to Sonoma. Starting in the 1850s, The Alameda became the site of distinguished residences belonging to many important and prominent families of Santa Clara County.

Wilmer and Dorothy Gross were recent Stanford graduates with bright futures. Wilmer was the only child of Frederick and Stella Gross, owners of the F.W. Gross & Son department store in downtown San José. The house was commissioned by Frederick Gross to be ready for the couple when they returned from their honeymoon.

Wilmer and Dorothy lived in the house less than a year, when Wilmer enlisted in the army, where he helped to form the California Grizzlies field artillery unit. The Grosses rented their house to David Low, founder of the Pratt-Low Cannery, and his wife Emily. Dorothy accompanied Wilmer to San Diego, where he was stationed, so she could be near him before he was sent overseas. The following year, Wilmer was sent to France, where he died of influenza.

Wilmer's death was a blow to his wife and parents. Frederick Gross, who reportedly never recovered from the death of his son, died in 1920. Dorothy did not return to live in her house; she sold it to the Lows and in 1921, she went to France with the American Committee for Devastated France to help with relief work for the war-torn country. She later remarried and moved to Texas. Wilmer's mother Stella Gross lived until the age of ninety-nine. After a long life of philanthropy, in 1966, she left the Stella B. Gross Charitable Trust, which today helps to fund nonprofits throughout San José.

In 1957, the house, on its fourth set of owners, was moved to the Rose Garden neighborhood in San José. Property values on The Alameda had increased greatly as its magnificent single-family residences were demolished or converted into commercial properties, and the owner wanted to sell the land and also to move the house to a residential neighborhood.

The Gross house is a distinctive example of the Dutch Colonial Revival style, a form of Colonial Revival marrying the Dutch Colonial gambrel roof with the features of American Revolutionary War architecture.

TOP: The porch is the focal point of the house. Higgins's distinctive multi-pillared porches appeared on several of the Wolfe & Higgins houses.

ABOVE: The entry hall of the Gross house shows the impressive staircase with its elaborate volute and curved railing.

RIGHT: The house being moved in 1957.

The style gained popularity in the late 1890s and continued well into the 1920s, when Sears and other catalog companies offered several versions of Dutch Colonial Revival kits. This style is not common in San José, and a number of the Dutch Colonial

TOP LEFT AND CENTER: Fireplace detail and front porch pillars. Dentil molding and inset panels on the fireplace reflect the design of the front porch. Higgins's practice, continued throughout the Wolfe & Higgins years, was to match the fireplaces with exterior elements such as the pillars on the front porch.

TOP RIGHT: Dining room with pocket doors in the Gross house. Pocket doors and angled corner built-in cabinets with arched windows are features that were repeated often in later Wolfe & Higgins houses.

ABOVE LEFT: The curved staircase railing and distinctive volute are elements that appear regularly in other Wolfe & Higgins buildings.

ABOVE RIGHT: Living room in the Gross house.

houses that do exist are those designed by William Higgins or Wolfe & Higgins.

The house's original character-defining materials include the symmetrical front façade with pitched gambrel roof and shed dormers, the elaborate central portico with classical columns and pilasters, the door surround with the fanlight and four-part multi-light doors, and most of the original interior features in the front rooms of the house.

Jane and Charles Polhemus House
San José

One of William Higgins's few still-standing buildings is a very large residence designed for the descendants of landowner and railroad scion Charles Bispham Polhemus. Polhemus possessed a mind-boggling amount of property. In the 1850s, he owned most of the Peninsula; one of his early estates later became the city of San Mateo, and other holdings became Atherton, Millbrae, and Menlo Park. He was responsible for bringing the railroad from San Francisco to San José, and in 1873, he moved to the corner of Stockton Avenue and Polhemus Street (today Taylor Street) in San José.

Charles Polhemus died in 1904 and his son George died in 1914, leaving grandson Charles B. Polhemus II in charge of the estate. When the family home burned down, Charles II hired William Higgins to design a new house, which was completed in 1916 as a very large seventeen-room residence in a Dutch Colonial Revival style.

In 1946, the house was sold and moved to the nearby Bellarmine College Preparatory, a private Jesuit secondary school. Now called Berchmans Hall, the building, originally used as a dorm for seniors, is the oldest building on the campus.

TOP: The Polhemus house being moved to Bellarmine College Preparatory in 1946.
Courtesy, History San José.

RIGHT: Today known as Berchmans Hall, the Polhemus house is the oldest building on the campus of Bellarmine College Preparatory.

Kittie and Charles Kimberlin House
San José

One of the last houses Higgins designed before going into business with Frank Wolfe was in 1917 for Charles and Kittie Kimberlin. The grand residence sits on a double corner lot in the Naglee Park neighborhood in San José.

Charles, born in 1864 in Santa Clara, was the son of the accomplished James Monroe Kimberlin, early settler of Santa Clara County, professor of languages at the University of the Pacific, and founder of the Kimberlin Seed Company of Santa Clara. Charles had taken over the seed company with his brother when their father died in 1904, and increased its success, turning it into an international company.

Kittie Kimberlin, born Katherine Andrews in West Virginia in 1871, married Charles in 1891. She became an active member of, and officer in, the Santa Clara Woman's Club, along with Lucy Higgins. Charles Kimberlin died in 1921 and Kittie's son Lloyd and his wife Dorothea lived in the house until about 1935, when it became the home of Ada and Dr. Clyde Wayland.

The house, with its repeated use of the arch, shows that Higgins was using elements such as arched doors and windows and decorative corbels before he partnered with Frank Wolfe. The Kimberlin house mixes many styles—a two-story Greek Revival porch with Tuscan columns

BELOW: The staircase in the Kimberlin house shares some features with that in the Gross house. The volute on the stair railing and turned balusters appeared regularly on Higgins staircases throughout the Wolfe & Higgins years.

BELOW RIGHT: The balustrade on the central front balcony matches the rooftop railing and the interior staircase.

RIGHT: An early photograph of the Kimberlin house shows the eclectic mix of styles that make up this unique residence. Used with permission of SJSU Library Special Collections and Archives.

BELOW RIGHT: The Kimberlin house today, after many years of restoration to bring it back to its original appearance. High trees cloak some of the view, but its grandeur still shows through.

and matching full-height pilasters supports a decorative rooftop railing. The same style pilasters and columns appear on the right wing of house. Dentil molding and turned spindles are used as ornamental elements. Above the front door, a balcony with slender turned spindles is supported by decorative corbels. Various details are inspired by Colonial Revival, Craftsman, and Italian Renaissance Revival architecture.

The right wing has a walled rooftop terrace with a pergola structure; its pillars support cross beams with contoured rafter tails. The two front windows on the first floor of the wing are arched, and on the side, a multi-paned arched glass door is flanked by two smaller arched side lights. The triple arch motif would become a mainstay of Wolfe & Higgins design.

BELOW LEFT AND RIGHT: Arched doors and windows in the Kimberlin house.

BOTTOM: Living room in the Kimberlin house.

Carl Jay Wolfe

Carl Jay Wolfe (1888-1931).

Carl Wolfe was born on January 16, 1888, in Newton, Kansas, where Frank and Nellie Wolfe had been living while Frank Wolfe was training under Illinois architect William L. Ross. Before Carl was a year old, the family, along with Frank's parents and siblings, moved to San José, California.

Carl grew up surrounded by and learning from architects and builders. By the time he was in his teens, his father was established in his career as a San José architect and was the senior partner in the well-known firm Wolfe & McKenzie. Carl's grandfather Jeremiah was locally known as a master builder, and his uncle Ernest Linwood was also fast becoming known as one of the best builders in the area.

At age seventeen, Carl Wolfe left to study art at Heidelberg University in Tiffin, Ohio, which he appears to have attended for two years. It is not known if he received a degree, but the training would certainly have helped him hone his design skills. Carl may have been sent to Ohio to stay with his parents' families, where he would be away from gossip caused by a scandal in which he was embroiled. In 1905, Carl and the Wolfe family were in the news as a tragic story played out. Carl's girlfriend Gladys Cunningham became pregnant and Carl ran away when both sets of parents pressured him to marry her. Gladys died while undergoing an abortion. Both her family doctor and the San Francisco doctor who performed the procedure were arrested and a search was made for Carl, although the search was dropped when it was ascertained that Carl was not legally liable.

After returning to San José in 1907, Carl started working for his grandfather Jeremiah in the construction business, under the name of Wolfe & Wolfe. While working with his grandfather, Carl had a chance to design some of the houses for their clients. In 1908, Carl Wolfe, only twenty years old, was the architect for both a bungalow in Naglee Park for hardware salesman Frank Gilger and his wife Dilea and a Craftsman house for Stephen and Kate Chase of the SH Chase Lumber Company.

BELOW: Carl Wolfe designed this house for Kate and Stephen Chase in 1908.

In 1907, Carl married Olga Eckstein, daughter of German immigrants. Olga, born in San Francisco, had lived most of her life in Mexico, where her parents had moved to start a coffee plantation. When her father died in 1904, the family returned to San José, where Olga attended San Jose Business College. Carl and Olga had three children: Delos (1908-1940), Linwood (born in 1910, he lived only two months), and Dolores (1912-2004).

In 1911, Carl went to work for his father as a draftsman. Frank Wolfe had just separated from partner Charles McKenzie, and there was a lot of work to be done. He made Carl an associate in 1912. (This firm, too, was informally called "Wolfe & Wolfe," although in city directories, it was listed as Frank Wolfe, Architect, with Carl's entry indicating that he was an associate at F.D. Wolfe.) Carl Wolfe is not on record as having received an architect's license from the state of California, which may be the reason he was not made a partner during his father's lifetime.

In 1917, Carl Wolfe separated from wife Olga. The divorce was finalized in 1918. Olga later died at the young age of thirty-six in 1925.

Although Carl had asked for an exemption from the draft due to the need to support his wife and children, he was denied the exemption. In 1917, shortly after being drafted, he joined the Marines. During this period, he met and married Faye Watts in 1918 in Montana.

After the war, Carl returned to San José to work in the newly formed firm of Wolfe & Higgins, where his job title was again Draftsman. Frank Wolfe died in October of 1926, and the firm of Wolfe & Higgins continued, with Carl Wolfe finally a partner. Some of the firm's most memorable buildings were done during the Carl Wolfe period, among them a grand residence for San José political boss Charles Bigley, the Packard Agency in San José, the San José Woman's Club, and, in 1931, the St. Helena Grammar School.

Carl Wolfe's last project was the grammar school in St. Helena. (See page 191.) He was working long hours on the plans and on July 2, 1931 at three o'clock in the morning, he was reportedly within hours of finishing when he was stricken with pain. He was taken to the hospital, where it was found he had peritonitis, an inflammation of the tissue that lines the abdomen. Doctors operated but were unable to save him. He was only forty-three.

The Wolfe architectural legacy, which had begun in 1888, the year Carl was born, had finally ended.

Frank Delos Wolfe &

William Ernest Higgins

1918-1926

ROOM ELEVATION
Scale ½" = 1'0"

SLIDING

FRONT ELEVATION
Scale ¼" = 1'0"

1918

The first full year of the Wolfe & Higgins partnership followed the United States' entry into World War I. Business was sparse for the architects.

Building was postponed nationwide, both because the government had asked the citizenry to refrain from building so as not to impede the war effort, and also because the cost of building materials was prohibitive because of the war. In October of 1918, Frank Wolfe and Warren Skillings represented local architects at a Santa Clara County committee meeting at which a representative from the federal government discussed the need to defer any building except that which was absolutely necessary. The attendees were told that the likelihood of getting a permit for a large job was remote.

Despite the restrictions set by the war, Wolfe & Higgins were able to work on thirteen projects, including a number of commercial buildings in downtown San José and a school in Cupertino. In Los Gatos, they converted the Rankin Building into the post office. The building, still standing today, may have been originally designed by Wolfe & McKenzie. The Rankin Building was one of two "business blocks," or large multi-business buildings commissioned by William Blackstone Rankin, a Los Gatos investor who also operated a number of large wineries and was manager of the California Wine Association.

Only two houses are on record as having been commissioned in 1918, for wealthy clients who may have been able to circumvent war restrictions. Both are reflective of the earlier work of Frank Wolfe: a large Craftsman for rancher Howard Tilton of Morgan Hill and a Prairie-style house for fruit merchant and bank president Ralph Tooker of Los Altos.

1918 saw the first of what became many of the partnership's automobile-related projects—a service station for the Bisceglia Brothers and a garage for the Alliance Land Company. Any type of business related to the automobile was becoming popular and necessary, and this turned out to be a niche specialty for Wolfe & Higgins as more and more commercial and residential garages and automobile showrooms were built. In the 1920s, their Spanish Revival style became the hallmark of the automotive industry in San José.

BELOW: The 1918 Los Gatos Post Office conversion. *Courtesy of the Los Gatos Library.*

BOTTOM: The original Rankin Business Block, built in 1902, may have been originally designed by Wolfe & McKenzie before it was renovated by Wolfe & Higgins in 1918. The Mission Revival building is still in use today in downtown Los Gatos. *Courtesy of the Los Gatos Library.*

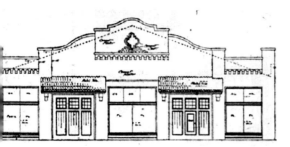

ABOVE: The original Letcher Garage was a Mission Revival design done by Wolfe & McKenzie in 1907.

RIGHT: In 1914, Frank Wolfe was hired to redesign the Letcher Garage into this Tudor style. *Courtesy, History San José.*

ABOVE: Frank Wolfe drawing of the 1916 garage for Dorrance & Farringon.

San José was not only a center for auto sales and repairs since 1900, but at one time had been the home of automobile manufacturing. In 1906, the Victory Motor Car Company, manufacturer of Sunset automobiles, and one of only two automobile factories on the Pacific Coast, moved to San José.

Frank Wolfe had been involved in designing buildings for the auto-motive industry since 1907, when Wolfe & McKenzie designed a new "garage" (automobile showroom and service station) for Clarence Letcher, the flamboyant king of automobile sales in San José and prob-ably all of California. Letcher, a Minnesota native who had moved to San José shortly after graduating from business college, opened the "Auto Depository" in 1901, the first garage in the West, and in 1902, he opened the first service station in the West, also in San José. The area around First Street in downtown San José became home to automobile sales and service, giving the dealers had more business than they could handle. Letcher had already outgrown two buildings when he hired Wolfe & McKenzie in 1907 to design a building that accommodated his expanding business. This garage, designed in the Mission style, became well-known as Letcher, a promotional genius, posted signs across California to point drivers to the San José location.

One project of which, unfortunately, no photographs remain, is a 1922 Wolfe & Higgins commission for Clarence Letcher's fourth garage. The architects were hired to design a state-of-the-art "auto palace" on the corner of First Street and St. James in San José. The new building would provide far more showroom, service, and office space than currently

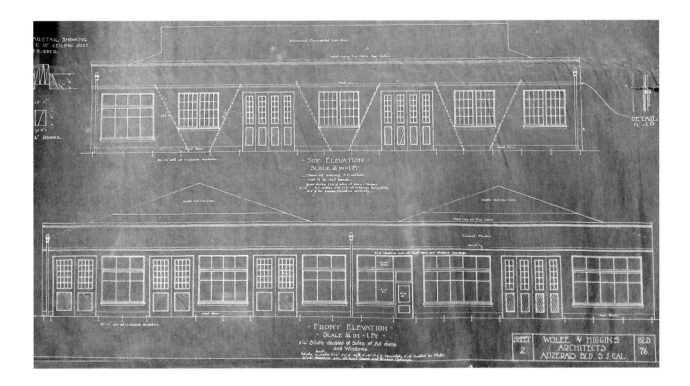

ABOVE: 1922 blueprints for the Albertson & Fisher garage. Courtesy, History San José.

RIGHT: In 1916, Frank Wolfe designed what the newspaper called a "highly artistic" and "palatial" garage for the Granger & De Hart company, distributors of Chevrolet motor cars. The building was considered to be one of the most modern and up-to-date of any in the automotive industry. Used with permission of SJSU Library Special Collections and Archives.

FAR RIGHT: Frank Wolfe's drawing of the Granger & De Hart garage.

existed. From an architectural standpoint, the new garage was of interest because it had no supports—the spans were said to be the longest of any existing local building.

The new garage opened in 1923 and construction continued through 1925, but unfortunately, Clarence Letcher was unable to make the most of his new building. On July 2, 1926, his wife Helen came to his workplace to confront him over his affair with a local hairdresser named Ann Bennet. After a short argument, Helen pulled a gun from her purse and shot Clarence and then killed herself. Clarence Letcher died the following day. The scandal was huge and the story continued in the news for days.

ABOVE: San José garage owner Henry Hoover followed the trend by adding ornamentation to his garage. Originally designed by Wolfe in 1913, it was remodeled in 1916.

BELOW: The Pichetti Brothers automobile showroom, built in 1930 in downtown San José. Used with permission of SJSU Library Special Collections and Archives.

Less than two years after Letcher's death, the Hollingsworth & Nash auto dealership bought the new building and Letcher's son George ran the business from the older Wolfe & McKenzie building. By the mid-1940s, the Wolfe & Higgins fourth garage had been re-adapted for use as county offices and was later demolished.

As the Spanish Revival style became symbolic of California architecture, it became the style of choice for automotive-related buildings in San José. Wolfe & Higgins designed buildings for Walter Curtner and attorney Robert Wright (1920), Albertson & Fischer (1922), Close & Close (1925), and Normandin & Campen (1927), to name just a few of the major dealers in San José. Their work culminated in the 1928 Packard Building in San José. (See page 170.) The magnificently restored Packard Building is one of the very few Wolfe & Higgins automobile-related buildings still standing.

1919

In January of 1919, San José was counting on a building boom. The effects of World War I could still be felt throughout the Santa Clara Valley. The war had officially ended November 11, 1918, and postwar cleanup continued into 1919. It had cost the country a great deal and resulted in an economic decline that was to grow into a nationwide recession by the early 1920s, but California, due to its thriving agriculture, oil, and entertainment industries, felt this decline less than did the rest of the country. The war effort had created improvements in mass-production and this would enable more houses to be built at a better level of quality, making a difference in home-building.

San José claimed to have an acute housing shortage. The local newspapers had always boasted of growth, and 1919 was no different, as articles informed would-be homeowners that even though building and labor costs were higher than ever, they were unlikely to go down, so now was the time to build. "Building is...the key of a community's prosperity and home building plays a very important part..." urged the *San Jose Mercury Herald*, noting that huge numbers of people were moving to San José and choice housing was becoming scarce. "People have too much money nowadays to live in old, tumbled down shacks" said a real estate salesman in a January 30 article called "BUILDING BOOM IS LOOKED FOR IN THIS CITY."

The article continued:

> As to the prospects of building, they are far better than they were two months ago. Two months ago, the architects were absolutely idle....A tour was made yesterday of the offices of the local architects and the professional men were found very hopeful. They said they were receiving visits almost daily from property owners who were thinking about building this year...."If half build who are talking about it, we will have all the work we can handle," said one architect.

For Wolfe & Higgins, business was much better than it had been during the previous year. They worked on at least twenty-five projects in 1919, a mix of commercial and residential work, much of it remodels. Perhaps in response to the purported need for more housing, many owners hired Wolfe & Higgins to design apartment buildings or convert single-family residences into multi-unit dwellings; this type of work soon became a mainstay of their business.

Some of Wolfe & Higgins's most distinctive houses were designed in 1919.

ABOVE: Walter Curtner hired Wolfe & Higgins to design this house in the Naglee Park neighborhood of San José in 1919.

RIGHT: The entry hall features two arches in the otherwise square house.

Belle and Walter Curtner/Sarah and Louis Richards House
San José City Landmark

Walter J. Curtner, real estate developer and executive at the Home Union, a general merchandise market in downtown San José, was a regular customer of Frank Wolfe at the time he commissioned a house in the Naglee Park neighborhood of San José. The son of wealthy rancher and land developer Henry Curtner, Walter had hired and continued to hire Wolfe for a number of projects for both himself and his father. His daughter Lydia, young wife of Los Gatos merchant J. Walter Crider, had also commissioned Wolfe in 1914 to design her home in Los Gatos, a building that is today one of Wolfe's most distinctive Prairie-style residences.

The Walter Curtners owned the Naglee Park home for a very short time, selling it to nearby neighbors Sarah and Louis Richards by 1922. It was said that Sarah Richards, who often walked past the house as it was being built, had begged Walter Curtner to sell it to her and her husband. The Richardses, Russian immigrants who had moved to San José in 1911 and owned the Saratoga Market, lived in the house until 1945.

RIGHT: Dining room in the Curtner-Richards house. Built-in cabinetry, coved ceilings, and egg-and-dart molding are found in the dining rooms of nearly all of the Wolfe Prairie houses and many of the Wolfe & Higgins houses also. The square columns on the credenza echo the columns on the exterior of the house.

The house, with its use of a myriad of styles, shows the influence of both Wolfe and Higgins. Its complex cubic shapes and horizontal orientation and square corner piers are reflective of Wolfe's Prairie era. The bow window is reminiscent of Wolfe & McKenzie.

Deep overhanging boxed eaves are supported by simple brackets, similar to some of the Wolfe & Higgins Italian Renaissance Revival-influenced houses. Except for the wide wraparound porch, the Curtner-Richards house has a facade much like that of the house designed for Ida and Peter Jordan the same year. (See page 63.) Slightly differing front windows on the left versus the right and the large porch on only the right side of the house give the house an asymmetry suggestive of Frank Wolfe's influence.

ABOVE: In 1914, Walter Curtner's daughter Lydia Crider commissioned this Prairie-style home from Frank Wolfe.

BELOW RIGHT: Fireplace in the living room of the Curtner-Richards house.

The Curtner-Richards house is possibly the only Wolfe & Higgins house with a wide wraparound porch; this one wraps around the right side of the house and merges into the porte-cochere. Large Tuscan columns set on the porch balustrades support an upper deck.

Joseph Eastwood Sr. House
Mountain View

In 1919, Joseph Eastwood Sr. moved with his daughter Mary and son Joseph Jr. to their new home in Mountain View. The Eastwood home is the first Wolfe & Higgins building known to have a tile roof. Tile roofs were still relatively uncommon, and this imposing two-story house would have been a showpiece, as it still is today, with its three-part tiled hipped roof, very deep eaves, and exposed protruding rafters. The focal point of the house is its massive front porch with hipped tiled overhanging roof supported by eight Tuscan pillars, one of the most ornate pillared porches of the Wolfe & Higgins era.

Joseph Eastwood was founder and president of the American Forge Company of San Francisco, an iron and steel-forging company that specialized in naval work. Widowed in 1904 with three young children, Joseph worked first as a blacksmith, then started a business called American Tool Works, which became the American Forge Company in 1910. The company continued to grow and became one of the largest steel-forging plants on the West Coast. Joseph Sr. died in 1931 and son Joseph Jr. and later grandson Joseph Eastwood III continued to run the family business.

ABOVE: Anna Irvine house in Sunnyvale. William Higgins had established his reputation with the Dutch Colonial Revival style. The Irvine house, with its steeply pitched side gambrel roof with three dormers, veers from tradition with its arched tripartite windows. The central porch features Higgins's signature pediment and set of Tuscan columns.

Anna Irvine House
Sunnyvale

At the end of April 1919, a small article in the *San Jose Evening News* noted that "Mrs. A.A. Irvine of Sunnyvale has joined the 'build a home now' colony." This was a reference to the pressure put on the public to buy and build in order to help strengthen the postwar economy.

Anna Irvine was recently widowed when she commissioned this house from Wolfe & Higgins. Originally from Ireland and Germany respectively, Felix and Anna Irvine had moved to Sunnyvale in 1910, where they bought ten acres on which to raise fruit. Felix died in March of 1919, and as soon as the will went through probate, Anna ordered her new home, in which she stayed until her death in 1956. No longer on ten acres, today the house sits closely surrounded by new construction.

Ida and Peter Jordan House
San José

In the winter of 1919, oculist Peter A. Jordan, his wife Ida, and their young son Philip moved into their new house on The Alameda in San José. The Alameda was, and until the middle of the twentieth century would continue to be, the most elegant street in San José, a tree-lined avenue of mansions that housed many of the wealthiest and most influential people in San José. Frank Wolfe and William Higgins had designed many homes on The Alameda, and they continued to do so throughout their careers.

The Jordan house, like the Curtner-Richards house, has a low hipped roof with boxed overhanging eaves supported by simple brackets with dentil molding at the roof-wall junction, as well as a porte-cochere with rooftop

ABOVE LEFT: The living room, used today as a conference room, still has original features such as a ceiling–high fireplace, high baseboards, and moldings.

ABOVE RIGHT: Staircase and entrance hall in the Jordan house.

RIGHT: The fireplace in the Jordan house living room is flanked by French doors. Dentil molding and curvilinear brackets tie it to the exterior of the house. The very high paneled baseboards had been a feature in nearly every house Frank Wolfe designed in the 1910s. The Jordan house was one of the last in which this was done.

terrace and half-circle wrought-iron railings at the upstairs windows supported by decorative corbels. The central porch is small with an arched pediment supported by Tuscan pillars.

The Jordan house is one of several fine residences done in what can be called Italian Renaissance Revival. This style, one of the earliest of the Mediterranean styles, had been around since the 1890s, becoming popular as more Americans visited Europe and saw the palaces of Italy. The typically symmetrical buildings feature low-pitched hipped roofs, often with very widely overhanging eaves supported by decorative brackets. Italian Renaissance Revival features made their way into the houses designed for Walter Curtner, Joseph Eastwood, and Peter Jordan, and later residences such as that for Selma and Fred Harvey in 1921. (See page 72.)

The building today is owned and used as office space by the Dunham Associates CPA firm.

ABOVE: The Sim house in the Rose Garden neighborhood of San José.

Marcella and Douglas Sim House
San José

In late 1919, Wolfe & Higgins designed this Tudor Revival residence for Douglas and Marcella Sim, a socially prominent young San José couple who were married in 1917, an occasion celebrated for weeks in the local society columns. The house was a gift to the recent newlyweds from Marcella's widowed mother, who lived on The Alameda almost directly behind the Sims' new home.

Marcella was the oldest daughter of Frederick and Marcella Spring Moore, owners of the Spring's Clothing Store, one of the oldest stores in downtown San José. When Marcella's father died unexpectedly in 1903 at

TOP: Living room in the Sim house.

ABOVE: Pocket doors lead into the Sim dining room.

BELOW RIGHT: The staircase in the entry hall of the Sim house shows the hand of William Higgins with its angled newel post and rounded stairs.

the age of forty-four, her mother became president and manager of Spring's.

Marcella Sim was active in both social and civic affairs. A tireless volunteer for the war effort, an elected trustee for her local district, and a renowned hostess, she was well-known throughout San José. In later years, she took over the management of Spring's from her mother.

Douglas Sim was the son of wealthy orchardist Kelso Sim, an English immigrant who had moved to California in 1882. In 1918, Douglas became one of the founders of the Santa Clara Valley Growers' Association, a cooperative organization dedicated to canning, preserving, drying, and packing fruits and vegetables. The organization had purchased thirteen acres of land in downtown San José and built what was believed to be the largest cannery in the world.

A 1919 item in the *San Jose Evening News* announced the impending completion of the Sims' new house: "It is plaster and English in architecture, with an interesting roof line." The Sim house is the first of a number of Tudor Revival houses designed by the firm of Wolfe & Higgins. The Sim house is devoid of adornment; its facade is flat with symmetrical paired front gables. The front doorway, set in an arched entry, is offset to the left; the asymmetrical front door was a favorite feature of Frank Wolfe.

The Sims and their two daughters lived in the house until 1938.

1920

As predicted, building increased in San José and Santa Clara County and business continued to grow for Wolfe & Higgins in 1920. Records show at least thirty-five projects during the year, with some significant commercial projects among their usual residential work. In May of 1920, Wolfe & Higgins were the architects for the Exposition of the Hundred Per Cent Club, held in downtown San José. The eight-day industrial exposition was enormous; more than 30,000 attended in a given day. The exposition featured industrial and residential machinery of all types, with its biggest section dedicated to the automobile.

In October of 1920, Wolfe & Higgins received a very large commission in Santa Clara. The Santa Clara Chamber of Commerce decided to build thirty houses around the city of Santa Clara, which they would sell on the "easy payment plan." (What this means is that there are probably thirty as-yet-identified houses in Santa Clara designed by Wolfe & Higgins!) Investors in the project

were some of the leading names in the city of Santa Clara: Robert Fatjo of the Bank of Italy (and owner of the Frank Wolfe-designed 1911 Mission Revival house in Santa Clara shown on page 33), W.F. Hayward of the Pacific Manufacturing Company, and George Fatjo of the Santa Clara branch of the Garden City bank.

Postwar construction in the area also meant focusing again on schools. An editorial in the *San Jose Evening News* urged voters to pass an upcoming bond to enlarge grammar and high schools, pointing out that

> When our present schools were built 12 years ago, there were 116 teachers in San Jose. Today there are 227. There were then 3023 elementary pupils. Today there are 5400. There were 616 high school pupils at that time. Today there are 1757.

ABOVE: The early work on schools resulted in some of Frank Wolfe's best Mission Revival school design. The Lowell School in San José, designed by Frank Wolfe, was enlarged in 1920.

RIGHT TOP: Frank Wolfe designed San José's Mission Revival Horace Mann School in 1916 and Wolfe & Higgins enlarged it in 1920.

RIGHT: Wolfe & McKenzie designed the original Grant School in San José in 1907 and Wolfe & Higgins expanded it in 1920.

When the bond passed, local architects such as Binder & Curtis, Charles McKenzie, and Louis Lenzen were commissioned to work on schools in the area. Wolfe & Higgins won eight school projects that year, not only in San José, but also in Fremont and Mountain View.

RIGHT: Ralph Berggren's house in the Rose Garden neighborhood in San José.

BELOW: In 1925, Wolfe & Higgins designed Ralph Berggren's Electrical Service shop in downtown San José (demolished). Used with permission of SJSU Library Special Collections and Archives.

Esther and Ralph Berggren House
San José

The house built for auto electrician Ralph Berggren includes features by now associated with Wolfe & Higgins—pediment set into a hipped roof, square pilasters framing the door, and wing wall with arched doorway. The low square piers with brick caps and window box are reminiscent of Frank Wolfe's Prairie-style buildings.

Five years after designing the Berggren house, in 1925, Wolfe & Higgins designed Berggren's electrical shop in downtown San José, since demolished.

RIGHT: This building, designed as an investment property for Dr. Thomas Blanchard, contains an apartment on each floor. Wolfe & Higgins had a thriving business designing duplexes and apartment buildings. The duplexes produced by the architects typically had a lack of symmetry that gave the appearance of a single-family residence, while providing distinctly different entrances for the two residences.

The Blanchard building has exterior stairs leading to the upper unit, a Spanish Revival feature applied more often in Southern California. External staircases are seen on only one other Wolfe & Higgins project, the Morris Atlas apartment complex done in 1928. (See page 156.)

Dr. Thomas Blanchard Apartments
San José

Dr. Thomas L. Blanchard had this two-apartment building built in downtown San José in the exclusive Hawthorne Place neighborhood, as an investment property. He and wife Miriam lived nearby.

Walter Curtner and Robert Wright Commercial Building
San José

This single-story concrete building with Mission Revival features was originally built as an automobile dealership among the automobile businesses that populated the First Street area of downtown San José. Walter J. Curtner, original owner of the Wolfe & Higgins house shown on page 59 and a regular customer of Frank Wolfe, partnered with attorney Robert Wright to commission this building. Wright later hired Wolfe & Higgins to design his 1922 home. (See page 91.)

RIGHT: The Curtner-Wright building, originally used as an automobile showroom, shows some of the decorative elements that became standard for the automobile trade in San José.

ABOVE: Wolfe & Higgins incorporated a number of Classical Revival features in the Growers National Bank of Campbell. The parapet screen on top is made of terracotta.

BELOW: Frank Wolfe designed Curry's Mission Revival building in 1913, across the street from the bank.

Growers National Bank (Benjamin Curry)
Campbell

In 1920, real estate developer Benjamin O. Curry hired Wolfe & Higgins to design the Growers National Bank in Campbell, an independent bank that Curry paid to have built and of which he was president. Built by Z.O. Field, one of the top contractors in the area, the bank catered to farmers and orchardists in the county; hence the name. Curry had previously hired Wolfe in 1913 to design a Mission-style building across the street in which he housed his real estate business.

Of Norwegian descent, B.O. Curry came to the United States in 1875 at the age of twenty-three, later marrying his wife Caroline (Carrie) with whom he had two daughters, Ethel and Myrtle. He settled in Campbell, where he was an active member of the community and a leader in local business. In addition to his real estate and banking contributions, he was an orchardist, school trustee, a founding director of the Central Santa Clara Fruit Company and a founding member of the local chapter of the Odd Fellows.

1921

In 1921, Wolfe & Higgins worked on more than forty projects, a mix of residential and commercial buildings and schools.

Sarah and James Baker House
Santa Clara

This Spanish Revival Santa Clara house was built for bricklayer James T. Baker and his wife Sarah, who lived here with their son Herbert. This house is constructed from hollow-core tile, or, as it was called in the 1920s, hollow tile. Hollow tile consisted of a terracotta building block with an interior made of hollow cells, resulting in a lightweight but strong building material that was, most importantly, fireproof. The blocks had a ribbed surface that helped stucco adhere. The Baker house has a brick foundation and front steps, most likely the work of original owner James Baker.

ABOVE: Hollow-tile house built for Sarah and James Baker.

BELOW: Alice Bassler house.

Alice Bassler House
San José

Alice Bassler commissioned this two-story Tudor Revival house in the Rose Garden neighborhood of San José. Bassler was director of women's physical education at the State Normal School, a job she took seriously—a proponent of physical culture and gymnastics, she took a year's leave in 1912 for specialized study in Europe and Asia. The Rose Garden

house was an investment for Bassler, who, never married, lived in downtown San José in her family home. Alice's parents probably instilled in their daughter an interest in real estate investment. Her father Joseph Bassler, a tinsmith and plumber, had made considerable investments in property and left a substantial estate when he died in 1895. Her mother, Alice Sr., owned residential and commercial property; one of her buildings, today known as the Bassler-Haynes Building, is listed as a Structure of Merit on the San José Inventory.

Ethel and Joseph Donovan House
San José

This Naglee Park house designed for clothing store salesman Joseph L. Donovan and his wife Ethel has the form and overhanging eaves of Wolfe's Prairie era. Eight Tuscan pillars support the large side porch.

ABOVE: Donovan house.

BELOW: The house designed for Fred and Selma Harvey incorporates many of the Wolfe & Higgins signature features: semi-circular balconies with wrought-iron railings and scrolled corbels, a massive porch with Tuscan pillars as the focal point, and a porte-cochere with rooftop terrace.

RIGHT: Balcony on the Harvey house.

BELOW RIGHT: The porte-cochere of the Harvey house is on the back, supported by square Prairie style pillars.

Selma and Fred Harvey House
Union City

Merchant Fred Harvey had this house built in Alvarado (today Union City), across the street from his store. The Harvey house has Italian Renaissance Revival features similar to the Curtner-Richards and Jordan houses of 1919. For the Harveys, Wolfe & Higgins added an elaborate multi-pillared front porch supporting an upper-story balcony and deeply set arched windows. A large wing with sleeping porch extends from the right side. Like those other two houses, there is a porte-cochere, in this case on the back of the Harvey house.

Today the Harvey house is used as office space.

Elsie and Harry Preston House
San José

Harry Preston was a real estate salesman who, with his wife Elsie, had several speculative houses built around San José. This attractive Spanish Revival bungalow with arched side entrance to the porch was built with his wife Elsie as a rental property.

ABOVE: The Preston spec house in San José.

BELOW: The Taormino house was the last of Frank Wolfe's large Prairie houses.

BOTTOM LEFT AND RIGHT: Two arches exist in the otherwise square Taormino Prairie house.

Frances and Sal Taormino/Assunta and Rocco Caputo House
San José City Landmark

In 1921, Wolfe & Higgins were commissioned to design a large Prairie-style house based on Wolfe's well-known Col house in San José. (See page 35.) Orchardist Filipo Taormino bought twenty acres of prune and apricot orchard in the rural area outside of San José and had the house built for his son Sal, the oldest of ten. Sal had returned from the war, was newly married, and his father wanted to keep him at home and in the family business. The newlyweds never moved into the house themselves, and the house eventually went into foreclosure. Rocco and Assunta Caputo bought it in 1931 and generations of their family lived there happily for the next seventy years.

Built at the very end of Wolfe's Prairie era, the house contains all of the features of Wolfe's best Prairie designs: flat roof and overhanging eaves with decorative fascia, stained glass clerestory windows with designs inspired by Frank Lloyd Wright, pendent tiles, and broad, open front porch with a low brick wall and square piers with contrasting caps. As a nod to the Wolfe & Higgins era, the house, otherwise consisting of straight lines, has two arches—a single arched doorway inside and a curvilinear arch surrounding the side porch.

Nellie and Frank Wolfe House
San José

Frank and Nellie Wolfe's last house, built in the Palm Haven neighborhood in San José, may have been inspired by, or in response to, the Dutch Colonial Revival homes designed by partner William Ernest Higgins. Not that Wolfe was a stranger to gambrel roofs—in his years with Charles McKenzie, the pair had designed a number of houses with cross-gambrel roofs.

The Wolfe house has a steeply pitched side gambrel roof with a single large shed dormer in front. The half-round entry portico with Ionic pillars was not new; Wolfe had first introduced a similar porch in 1903 on a house for Irene and Arthur Chambers. Dentil trim surrounds the house under the eaves. The first floor of the house is constructed from reinforced concrete, a material of interest to Wolfe, who had obtained a patent the same year his house was built for a concept for reinforcing concrete with tubular air pockets within. The original house had radiant floor heating,

ABOVE: Ionic pillars on the Wolfe house frame the tall trees of the Palm Haven neighborhood.

a novel concept in 1921, and one that Wolfe may have been one of the first to utilize. Frank Lloyd Wright had championed radiant floor heating since he discovered it in Japan in 1905, but it was not until the 1930s that Wright used it as a standard feature in his Usonian homes.

ABOVE: The final home of Frank and Nellie Wolfe was this house in Palm Haven.

RIGHT: Wolfe & McKenzie designed this house with a cross-gambrel roof for Thomas and Leonie Tormey in 1904.

Frank and Nellie Wolfe moved from their nearby Prairie-style home in which they had lived since 1912. After more than thirty years of moving, they had found their final home, with Frank living there until his death in 1926, and Nellie outlasting him another thirty-six years. Palm Haven, which had opened in 1914 to great

fanfare, prided itself on its architectural standards. "The building restrictions are to be rather severe... and those not caring to conform to a certain artistic standard will be practically barred from buying in this tract..." noted an article in the San José newspaper. Architects were available to prospective buyers to help them with sketches and estimates. Frank

TOP LEFT: Staircase in the Wolfe house.

TOP RIGHT: Entrance hall in the Wolfe house showcases the multi-paned double doors with sidelights.

ABOVE: The dining room has a coved ceiling with egg-and-dart molding. Egg-and-dart appears in nearly all of Wolfe's dining rooms.

RIGHT: The living room has double rows of egg-and-dart molding and a high fireplace.

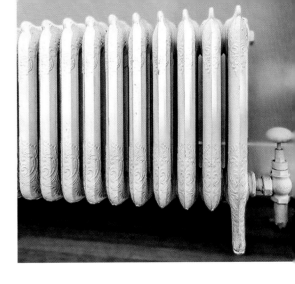

RIGHT: The original radiators in the Wolfe home still work and add a decorative note throughout the house. The house also was ahead of its time with original radiant floor heating, no longer existing.

BELOW: This house designed for Georgia Andrews was one of the first houses built in the Palm Haven Residence Park.

BOTTOM: Rose and Joseph Aeillo's house in Hanchett Park.

Wolfe, as one of San José's leading architects, had designed two of the original four houses featured in Palm Haven, a Mission Revival house for socialite Georgia Andrews and a Prairie style house built by and for his brother E.L. Wolfe in 1913. (See page 90.)

The Wolfe & Higgins partnership was responsible for many of the houses in and near Palm Haven. Members of the family lived there, including the Wolfes' daughter Edith and her husband, engineer and cannery executive Warren Rice. Frank Wolfe's brother E.L. and his family lived in Palm Haven until the late 1930s. Carl Wolfe also bought and sold and built in Palm Haven, living in at least four houses in the area.

1922

There was an increase in business for the firm in 1922, with records of fifty-eight projects, several of them large residences for influential locals. It was in 1922 that Wolfe & Higgins settled on what became their signature style, Spanish-influenced and ornate. Thanks to a highly visible commission from socialite Grace Spencer Hall (see page 80), which was completed early in the year, Wolfe & Higgins were to become known for this style. By the end of 1922, they were working almost exclusively in Spanish Revival and would continue to do so until the end of the partnership ten years later.

Rose and Joseph (Guiseppi) Aiello House
San José

Joseph and Rose Aiello were born in Italy and moved to California when both were young children. Joseph became a citizen in 1918 so he could enlist in the army when the United States entered World War I; he later became a wholesale vegetable dealer. The one-story Aiello house, built in the Hanchett Park neighborhood of San José, has an elaborate entrance similar to that on Frank Wolfe's own house (see page 74), with six Tuscan columns supporting a semicircular railed balcony.

Clara and Matthew Arnerich House
San José

Real estate salesman and city councilman Matthew Arnerich and his wife Clara lived in this house in downtown San José, an interesting mix of a number of the favorite design ideas of Wolfe & Higgins. The form, projecting side wings, overhanging eaves, horizontal orientation, inset panel trim, and pillars with contrasting caps are all features of Wolfe's Prairie era. The front entrance with its arched pediment and Tuscan columns reflects the ornate porches William Higgins had been designing since before he went into partnership with Wolfe. The escutcheons are elements that appear often in the firm's Spanish Revival work. Wide French doors with sidelights on either side of the front entrance and large front picture windows create a wide expanse of glass that merges the indoors with the outdoors.

Marion and David Atkinson House
San José

David Atkinson was the younger brother of real estate mogul William L. Atkinson, a long-standing client of Frank Wolfe's. (Older brother William was owner of a Wolfe Prairie house and in 1925, commissioned the Realty Building, where Wolfe & Higgins established their office.) David Atkinson worked for his brother as a real estate salesman and his wife Marion worked as a teacher when they lived in this Tudor Revival home in the Hester Park neighborhood of San José.

ABOVE RIGHT: The Arnerich house is a variation of Wolfe's Prairie style with Mediterranean Revival details.

RIGHT: The Atkinson house.

BELOW TOP: One of the many Spanish Revival one-story houses commissioned by Adolph Goldstein in the Hanchett Park neighborhood in San José. He lived in this house, with its two sets of triple arches, while buying land in the neighborhood.

BELOW CENTER: Living room in the Goldstein house.

BOTTOM AND RIGHT: Two of the many houses built by Adolph Goldstein in Hanchett Park.

Adolph Goldstein Houses
San José

Adolph Goldstein was a San José builder/carpenter who, like many other builders in the area, regularly used Wolfe & Higgins as his architects. Originally from Hungary, the twenty-seven-year-old Goldstein came to California in 1904, intending to send for his wife and infant daughter when he got settled. He worked first as a pattern maker and over time, was able to go into business for himself as a carpenter.

Soon after his arrival in the United States, his wife died in Hungary and his daughter Elisabeta was sent to live with her grandmother. Finances, and then World War I and strict immigration laws prevented him from seeing his daughter until she was eighteen, when the San José YWCA helped him bring her to the United States in 1922.

By 1922, Goldstein was on his way to becoming a successful contractor and real estate investor. He bought land in prestigious neighborhoods such as Hanchett Park and Palm Haven and built small, elegant homes, most or all of which appear to be Wolfe & Higgins designs. He sometimes lived in these houses for a year or two before moving to another. In the 1920s, he and his second wife Bertha, whom he married in 1911, moved to a permanent home in Los Gatos.

Grace Spencer Hall House
San José

Grace Spencer Hall's striking house on The Alameda in San José is almost certainly the first building to which Wolfe & Higgins applied Churrigueresque ornamentation. The elaborate door surround is the impressive focal point of this two-story building. Twisted pilasters topped by large finials frame the arched doorway. A large arched hood-molded window with a projecting wrought-iron radius balcony is centered above the entrance.

The Hall residence is the first of many of the large Spanish Revival residences designed by Wolfe & Higgins, with symmetrical or part-symmetrical center sections with a series of stepped flat fronts, their facades broken by arched doors and windows, wrought-iron railings, and ornamental plaster or terracotta. The central flat roof with its edging of barrel tile steps down and then slopes on both sides to provide visual interest, as do asymmetrical wings.

ABOVE: The house designed for socialite and real estate developer Grace Spencer Hall was responsible for helping to establish Wolfe & Higgins as the foremost local architects of the Spanish Revival style.

Grace Spencer Hall was the daughter of renowned district attorney and judge Francis E. Spencer. In 1894, she married physician J. Underwood Hall, but the couple became estranged in 1918 and were divorced two years later. In 1916, Grace Spencer Hall had hired William Higgins to help renovate her family home, so she turned to Wolfe & Higgins when she wanted a new house after her divorce. Plans were underway at the end of 1921 and the house was completed early in 1922.

Hall's house on The Alameda in San José elicited much excitement in the local newspapers and undoubtedly helped establish Wolfe & Higgins as the leading local designers of the Spanish Revival style. Said a January 2, 1922 article in the *San Jose Mercury Herald*:

> Following closely in all details the ideas of the early Spanish fathers in the building, one of the most attractive houses in the west will soon be completed in this city....the residence to be erected for Mrs. Hall is truly Spanish with touches of the Aztec which they used.
>
> "I am very proud of the plans for the house" said Mrs. Hall... "The place will be truly Spanish yet the interior will be as modern as it can be built."

The Hall residence, today a law office, still stands out on The Alameda. It has been renovated in the interior and has an addition on the back, but the front exterior is faithful to its original design.

Verna and Theodore Hansen House

San José

This one-story Prairie-style house was built in San José's Hanchett Park neighborhood for fruit machinery assembler Theodore Hansen and his wife Verna. The Hansen house has many of the characteristics of the Prairie houses for which Frank Wolfe had become so well-known since 1912—deep overhanging eaves and large square pillars and low front wall with contrasting caps. Instead of the standard flat or low hipped roof of Wolfe's Prairie era, however, the Hansen house has a low gabled roof, clipped in the front and back and accented by protruding rafter tails and a strip of three latticed vertical windows. The clipped roof, also called a jerkinhead roof, was a feature that Wolfe & Higgins used many times over the next years.

RIGHT: The Hansen house in San José incorporates some of the Prairie features of Frank Wolfe's best-known work.

Mary Hawkins House
Hollister

Throughout his career, Frank Wolfe worked regularly for clients in Hollister and the rural areas surrounding it. Hollister, today with a population of around 35,000, was founded in 1874 as the county seat of San Benito County. In the 1890s through the 1920s, its population grew as people unfazed by the fact that it lay on the southern end of the Calaveras fault established year-round or country homes there.

Today, the city has five listings on the National Register of Historic Places, including the downtown Hollister Historic District and the Monterey Street Historic District. These districts contain buildings designed by some of the best local architects of their day.

Hollister founder Thomas S. Hawkins was largely responsible for Hollister's interest in fine architecture. He and his family commissioned

RIGHT: Pocket doors with arched panes lead from the dining room into the living room in Mary Hawkins's house.

BELOW LEFT: Watsonville architect William Weeks was one of many excellent local architects whose work is represented in Hollister. He designed several buildings there, including the Hazel Hawkins hospital, a memorial to T.S. Hawkins's beloved nine-year-old granddaughter who had died five years earlier from appendicitis. Today the building is used as office space.

BELOW RIGHT: In 1908, Wolfe & McKenzie designed this house for Hollister couple George and Gertrude Wapple. Because of the couple's influence, Wolfe went on to do a lot of work in Hollister and San Benito County.

TOP: The Mary Hawkins house in Hollister. Decorative chimneys are standard features in many Spanish Revival buildings. The chimney echoes the triple-arch theme that is repeated through the house.

ABOVE: The pilasters on the wood fireplace in the living room match the design of the porch exterior.

RIGHT: Living room in the Hawkins house.

ABOVE RIGHT: The Hawkins dining room features three arched windows over built-in cabinets with leaded-glass panes. Arched glass doors lead to the front yard.

BELOW: The second fireplace is in the Hawkins dining room.

many of the town's most outstanding buildings. In 1922, Wolfe & Higgins were hired to design a home for T.S. Hawkins's unmarried niece Mary.

Wolfe's reputation was already well established in Hollister at the time he and Higgins designed the Hawkins house. In 1908, Wolfe & McKenzie had designed homes for Julia and Dr. Joseph O'Donnell and pharmacist George Wapple and his wife Gertrude. (Today the Wapple residence houses the San Benito County Historical Association.)

Mary Hawkins's house is a Spanish Revival one-story residence with a blue tile roof, cross-gabled with a projecting front covered entrance offset to the left. All of the windows and nearly all of the doors in the house are arched, and triple arches are repeated throughout the structure. The front porch features three large arches framed by twisted spiral columns. The front entrance is an arched door flanked by two arched windows of the same height as the door. To the right of the porch, a double-arched door leads from the dining room to the outdoors. An arched window on the front right of the house features a decorative balustrade. The chimney continues the theme with a triple-arch design.

Opal and Stanley Hiller Sr. House
San José

One of Wolfe & Higgins's most distinctive residential designs is the two-story Spanish Revival house designed for engineer and inventor Stanley Hiller Sr. and his wife Opal in San José's Hanchett Residence Park.

At the time, Stanley Hiller was founder and president of Pacific By-Products, a company whose primary purpose was to convert fruit pits into charcoal. Less than three years after commissioning the San José house, the Hillers moved to Alameda County, where Hiller launched a number of other businesses. The Hillers' son Stanley Hiller Jr., born in 1924, went on to gain fame as a prodigy aviation pioneer, designing his first helicopter at age sixteen.

The Hillers sold the house to Stella and Harry Morris. Stella was the daughter of Leopold Hart, founder of the well-known Hart's Department Store in San José, and Harry was owner of a large hay and grain company. The Morrises stayed in the house until Stella's death in 1939.

BELOW: The Hiller house, with its enormous entry arch with rope trim and twisted columns, radius balconies and grillework, and stepped roof heights is among the most outstanding of Wolfe & Higgins's residential designs.

Bertha and Frederick Lyne House
San José

Frederick Lyne was owner of the Lyne Drug Company, a successful store on North First Street in San José, a site of thriving businesses and elegant homes. Lyne and his wife Bertha lived in this large two-story residence with a broad covered front porch with a triple arch entrance. Decorative elements include dentil molding under the eaves and an upper central and porch grilles made of turned wood balusters.

Today, the building is used as a medical office.

TOP: The striking Lyne residence was built close to Frederick Lyne's business.

ABOVE: Front porch of the Lyne house.

Ivy and Harold McKenley House
San José

This Spanish Revival house with triple arched windows, twisted spiral columns, and arcaded asymmetrical porch entry was designed for Ivy and Harold McKenley in the Naglee Park neighborhood of San José. Harold D. McKenley was a partner in the McKenley-Glans Furniture Company in downtown San José. The following year, his partner George Glans commissioned a Tudor-style home from Wolfe & Higgins. (See page 104.)

Stella and Baron Merchant House
San José

This one-story house built in San José's Naglee Park for Associated Oil Company clerk Baron Merchant and wife Stella has a steep pitched jerkinhead roof (a gable roof on which the peaks of the gable ends are clipped off with a small hip) and a large covered porch on the side. The front porch is also clipped, with the arched entry extending above the roof line.

TOP: Ivy and Harold McKenley house.

ABOVE CENTER: Stella and Baron Merchant house in Naglee Park.

ABOVE: Harriet Moore house.

Harriet Moore House
San José

Designed for widow Harriet Moore, this one-story Spanish Revival house in the Palm Haven neighborhood of San José was, when built, featured in the local newspaper because of its Spanish detailing and its singular raftered pergola built into the left side of the house under the roof eaves, with doors opening from it into the house. Today, the pergola has been closed in and some renovations have been made, but the house maintains its original charm with rich exterior decoration and triple-arched windows and arcaded entry.

Grace and Harold Philbrick House
Morgan Hill

Howard and Grace Philbrick had moved to Morgan Hill from the North Willow Glen neighborhood of San José, where Howard worked for the post office and Grace was a nursing supervisor for the State Board of Health. They commissioned a house similar to that of Matthew Arnerich, blending Mediterranean and Prairie features.

Angela and Claude Seifert House
San José

Claude Seifert was a salesman working for his father's automobile retail and service business when he and wife Angela had this Spanish Revival house built in the Rose Garden neighborhood of San José. It is perhaps the

first instance of what would become a common Wolfe & Higgins feature, a focal point large round arched window with wide vertical bead-and-reel molding on the mullions separating the window panes. Above the arched window is an ornate Arabesque attic vent.

Venetia Apartments (A. Clyde Alexander)
San José

Arthur "Clyde" Alexander was one of the many developers and builders who used Wolfe & Higgins. Originally from Santa Clara, where he had excelled at baseball, football, and track in high school, Alexander worked as a real estate salesman before quitting to enlist in the army to fight in World War I. After returning home from the war, he went into business for himself as an active investor and builder who advertised himself as "The Builder of Better Bungalows." The Venetia apartment building was one of the first buildings Alexander developed.

Partial to the Spanish Revival style, in the 1920s, Alexander built this type of house all over San José. He frequently used Wolfe & Higgins, but sometimes built them without an architect, perhaps using the Wolfe & Higgins plans he had already paid for. Alexander's "better bungalows" can be found throughout the historic neighborhoods in San José. In later years, A. Clyde Alexander was responsible for developing some of the largest residential neighborhoods in San José's Willow Glen.

RIGHT: A. Clyde Alexander's Venetia Apartments.

Marie and E.L. Wolfe House
San José

Frank Wolfe's brother, master builder Ernest Linwood "E.L." Wolfe (1870-1953), was the contractor on many of the most important buildings designed by Frank Wolfe throughout his career. E.L. Wolfe, like the rest of the Wolfe clan, was also an active real estate investor, buying land and building many houses on spec. He regularly showcased his skills by building and living in houses designed by Frank Wolfe.

In 1913, E.L. and his wife Marie had lived in one of the first Wolfe Prairie houses in the Palm Haven Residence Park in San José, staying there for nearly nine years until they decided to build this Spanish Revival bungalow also in Palm Haven. E.L. Wolfe went on to build and live in a number of houses in Palm Haven before moving to Santa Clara in 1940.

This Wolfe home features the elements that became standard on many of the Wolfe & Higgins Spanish Revival houses: a pyramid hipped roof, triple arches with a higher central arch and twisted spiral columns with Ionic capitals, wrought-iron window trim, decorative balusters that suggest Spanish grillework, and covered arcaded porch.

BELOW: From 1913 to 1922, E.L. and Marie Wolfe lived in this Prairie house, designed by Frank Wolfe and built by E.L.

BELOW RIGHT: E.L. and Marie Wolfe house in San José's Palm Haven neighborhood.

Kate and Robert Wright House
San José

Richly decorated with Churrigueresque door and window surrounds, wrought-iron balconies, and twisted spiral and Tuscan columns, the Wright house is one of the most distinctive residences of the Wolfe & Higgins era. This design was reused later in 1925 for the Dudfield family of Palo Alto with minor differences. (See page 128.)

Robert Mills Wright was forty-five years old and one of the best-known attorneys in San José when Wolfe & Higgins designed this house for him and his wife Kathryn (Kate). Robert Wright had partnered with Walter Curtner earlier to hire Wolfe & Higgins to design an auto showroom. (See page 69.)

Since 1905, when Wright was still a law clerk, the Wrights had been living on North First Street in downtown San José, but in 1922, garage owner Clarence Letcher persuaded the Wrights to sell their house to him so he could demolish it for a new state-of-the-art garage designed by Wolfe & Higgins.

TOP AND ABOVE: Ornamental details of the windows, doors, and balconies that comprise the Wright house.

RIGHT: The *San Jose Mercury Herald* described the entrance hall in the Wright house as "a joy forever."

PREVIOUS PAGE SPREAD: The Wright house, restored by its current owners, is as impressive today as it was when built in 1921.

ABOVE LEFT: The living room has floor-to-ceiling arched windows on three sides.

ABOVE RIGHT: Breakfast room.

BELOW LEFT: The dining room's three full-height arched windows face onto the front yard.

BELOW RIGHT: Entryways in the Wright house have massive frames with inset panels and flared caps. The matching fireplace can be seen through the doorway.

The Wrights responded by commissioning a grand residence from Wolfe & Higgins, perhaps more in keeping with their elevated social status. The house was featured in the *San Jose Mercury Herald*, which said:

> Modified Spanish, with a touch of Italian and a mere hint of pueblo and Aztec design, sets off the R.M. Wright residence as one of the most handsome homes in the city…So skillfully have flat surfaces been handled, that the nearly 100-foot width of the R.M. Wright home …seems a broad canvas broken by touches of artistry.

The Wrights lived in the house for more than thirty years. After Kate died around 1950, Robert continued to practice law and live in the house until his death in 1954.

1923

As business continued to improve for the firm, 1923 brought well over sixty projects, including a number of multi-unit dwellings—duplexes and apartment buildings, sometimes from a conversion of a single-family home.

Sophie and H. Lysle Austin House
San José

Henry "Lysle" Austin was secretary of the Bean Spray Pump Company, which in 1928 became Food Machinery Corporation (FMC), its name today. Austin was an active member of many civic organizations, including the San José Chamber of Commerce and Community Chest, and was on the board of directors of the YMCA, head of the Hundred Per Cent Club, and treasurer of the local chapter of the Odd Fellows.

The Austin house has a number of features that add to its distinctive style: a steep jerkinhead roof and an eyebrow portico with dentil trim, extending above the eave. A wing on the left side contains a deep porch with Tuscan pillars. This house is a variation on that built for the Merchants in 1922, shown on page 87.

RIGHT: Sophie and H. Lysle Austin commissioned this house in the Willow Glen neighborhood of San José.

ABOVE RIGHT: Side view of the Austin house's clipped roofs. Wolfe & Higgins produced a number of houses with jerkinhead roofs.

Myrtle and Charles Berman House
San José

ABOVE: Berman house in Hanchett Park.

This flat-roofed Spanish Revival home built in the Hanchett Residence Park in San José for traveling salesman Charles N. Berman and his wife Myrtle, incorporates a great number of the Spanish Revival elements in Wolfe & Higgins's repertoire, giving visual interest to a two-bedroom symmetrical house. Small eaves edged with barrel tiles are trimmed with dentil molding, and the facade presents two pairs of arched windows, stucco appliqués and terracotta ornamentation in the form of escutcheons, scrollwork, arched molding surrounding the door, and two rosettes on the parapet.

ABOVE LEFT: The De Sando apartment not long after it was first built. Recessed arches above the windows provide a Palladian form without the expense of making custom arched windows; the same is true of the front door, where a deeply recessed arched entrance over a square door gives it the look of an arched door. Used with permission of SJSU Library Special Collections and Archives.

ABOVE RIGHT: The De Sando apartment has changed very little today.

De Sando Apartments (Michael De Sando)
San José

Grocer Michael De Sando's only known foray into real estate development resulted in this handsome Wolfe & Higgins Spanish Revival apartment building in downtown San José. An eave edged with barrel tile projects from the front facade; narrowly spaced curvilinear rafter tails are exposed beneath the eave, suggesting the Italian Renaissance Revival features on some of their earlier buildings. The central flat roof is separated from sloping left and right sides by square rooftop pillars with urn-shaped finials.

Carrie and Frank Dreischmeyer House
San José

Built for Frank and Caroline (Carrie) Dreischmeyer in the Willow Glen neighborhood of San José, this one-story Spanish Revival house features a Churrigueresque entrance ranking with the best of the Wolfe & Higgins residences such as the Grace Spencer Hall house shown on page 80 and the Kate and Robert Wright house shown on page 91.

Frank Dreischmeyer was an attorney from the well-to-do Dreischmeyer family, which owned most of the brick-making business in San José. Carrie was daughter of orchardist John Addison Campbell, who owned eleven acres in Willow Glen. The couple married in 1899 and moved in with the widowed Campbell in his home at the edge of the orchard. Campbell died in 1901.

Frank Dreischmeyer had financial difficulties, and in 1913, it was discovered that he had been embezzling money from a number of his clients for some years. He was remorseful and accepted his fate without complaint; he pleaded guilty to embezzlement and forgery and was disbarred and sentenced to eight and five years concurrently in San

BELOW LEFT: The Dreischmeyer house has one of the finest examples of a Wolfe & Higgins Churrigueresque door surround. Dentil molding, a favorite feature of both Wolfe and Higgins, surrounds the exterior of the house.

RIGHT: The arched front door as seen from the inside.

BELOW RIGHT: The large focal window in the Dreischmeyer house is a segmental arched multi-paned window with acorn finials and recessed panel trim. A variation of this window is on the Glans house built in the same year, shown on page 104.

Quentin. Said the thirty-nine-year-old Dreischmeyer,

I am glad I have a chance to get this off my mind. Every time I have met an officer of the law on the street, for months, I have had a horrible fear that he might lay his hand on my shoulder and tell me to go with him.

Dreischmeyer gained parole after two years and eight months and returned home to take over his father-in-law's orchard. The couple lived out their lives quietly.

In 1923, the Dreischmeyers hired Wolfe & Higgins to design a new house, richly appointed with features in the newly popular Spanish Revival style, on the property shared with the John Addison Campbell house. It is unclear if the couple ever lived in the house; well into the 1940s, the house was occupied by a tenant while the Dreischmeyers lived in the house that had belonged to Carrie's father.

PREVIOUS PAGE SPREAD: The Dreischmeyer house.

TOP: The Dreischmeyer living room.

ABOVE AND RIGHT: The fireplace has tiles made by master tilemaker Ernest Batchelder of Pasadena. The musician corbels above can also be found in the famous Pasadena house that architects Greene & Greene designed for James Culbertson.

ABOVE: Gertrude Gardiner apartment building as it appeared in the April 1923 issue of *The Architect and Engineer*.

Gertrude Gardiner Apartments
Stanford

In 1923, tile roofs were still a fairly new phenomenon in Northern California. In the April 1923 issue of *The Architect and Engineer*, an article called "Tile Roofs" featured several Spanish Revival residences in Northern California. The title page showed a picture of the very new apartment building at Stanford designed by Wolfe & Higgins for Gertrude Gardiner, the matron of the Roble Residence Hall. The article gives some insight into the appeal of Spanish Revival. Wrote author W.O. Raiguel:

> The Victorian era set up new standards. Mathematical exactness of form and color became symbols of perfection, and the materials of common use lost the charm and beauty of human imperfection. New and horrible forms were invented, miracles of cheapness and standardization making their appeal to the mind rather than to the heart. In the last few years the pendulum has been swinging back, and manufacturers are now producing in quantity roof tiles of burned clay having a wide kiln variation in color...burned clay seems to retain its sympathy with mother earth and take its place easily and naturally in Nature's setting, its tone at once contrasting and blending with its surroundings. It has the artist's touch of sincerity, is never forced or discordant, and just naturally "belongs."

Wolfe & Higgins began drawing the plans for the Gardiner Apartments in 1921, after Stanford's Board of Trustees approved a lease for the lot between two sorority houses. Completed in 1923, the stucco building contained four apartments with a four-car garage behind the building. During Gardiner's ownership, the building was enlarged to contain seven apartments—a two-story addition with two studio apartments was added to one side, and a cottage was built in the back.

The building has changed very little throughout the years. Three large round arches extend across the first floor; the center arch is the building's entrance and to the left and right are huge windows. On the second floor, a set of three narrower arched windows with twisted spiral pilasters between them is centered above the entrance. The interior of the elegant building remains largely intact as well, with a common sitting room with fireplace and a grand staircase leading to the upper floor; its railing ending in a volute resembling that in the Gross-Low house that Higgins designed in 1916. (See page 42.) The four original apartments retain many original features: hammered glass, oak floors, arched interior doors, pocket doors, and built-in cabinets. Each apartment has a fireplace with a different surround and mantel.

Gertrude Gardiner (1869-1961) came to San José from Illinois as a young child. She learned about real estate speculation and land development

TOP: The Gardiner Apartments are still in use today as apartments on the Stanford campus.

ABOVE: Fountain in the back yard of the Gardiner Apartments.

RIGHT: The cottage in the back is where John F. Kennedy lived in 1940. *Photographs on this page and next by Sunny Scott.*

from her father and both she and her sister Nellie bought and sold land in San José and later Palo Alto. From 1899 to 1924, Gardiner worked as matron of Roble Hall on the Stanford campus. Before her death in 1961, she established the Gertrude Gardiner Scholarship, which is still awarded.

Unit 7, the cottage in the back yard, had many tenants who were well-known in Stanford's academic circles, but its most famous tenant by far was John F. Kennedy. In 1940, Kennedy audited classes at Stanford and rented Gertrude Gardiner's back-yard cottage.

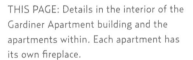

THIS PAGE: Details in the interior of the Gardiner Apartment building and the apartments within. Each apartment has its own fireplace.

Sidney and George Glans
San José

George Glans was a partner in the McKenley-Glans Furniture Store in downtown San José. (Partner Harold McKenley also had a Wolfe & Higgins house, shown on page 87.) The Glans home has a dramatic focal point in its multi-paned segmental arched window with tear-drop-shaped finials. An arched entranced and shaped wing wall frame a front walled courtyard.

ABOVE: The Glans house is in the Naglee Park neighborhood in San José.

BELOW RIGHT: The Kocher duplex reflects the Spanish Colonial style, with a flat roof with parapet and porch with shed roof. The windows are smaller in this building than they are in the other Wolfe & Higgins houses of this era, following the Spanish Colonial style.

George Kocher Duplex
San José

George Kocher was one of many building contractors and real estate developers who used Wolfe & Higgins for a number of projects. In 1923, Kocher had this duplex built as an investment property. This building is the first example of a style that evolved to become a favorite of Carl Wolfe's—a Spanish Colonial-style flat-roofed structure with a shed roof supported by simple timber posts, extending over a walled wide front porch. A single arched front door leads into a hallway that connects the two homes.

Vera and Frank Pascoe Triplex
San José

Plumber Frank E. Pascoe and his wife Vera commissioned this building in downtown San José as a three-family house; they lived in one of the units. Today, it has been divided into apartments. This building, with its completely flat roof and flat front, uses ornamental moldings and balconies to provide considerable visual interest.

Rogers Apartments (Katie Rogers)
San José

This ornate apartment building with twisted spiral columns and wrought-iron grillework was built for widow Katie Rogers.

Pearl and Herbert Schulze House
Hollister

This Tudor Revival house, designed for Pearl and Herbert A. Schulze on their ranch, is reminiscent of the Sim house shown on page 65, with its double gables. The huge round four-part arched door helps identify it as a Wolfe & Higgins home as well. Pearl Hawkins Schulze was the granddaughter of T.S. Hawkins, the founder of Hollister.

TOP: The Pascoe residence was built as a triplex.

ABOVE: Katie Rogers apartment building.

RIGHT: The Pearl and Herbert Schulze house was built on their ranch outside of Hollister. The two wings of the Schulze house angle out from the center of the house.

Mabel and Urban Sontheimer House
San José

The Sontheimer house in San José's Palm Haven neighborhood was built by E.L. Wolfe, with a design similar to E.L. Wolfe's own house shown on page 90. Urban Sontheimer (1888-1966), with a 1914 law degree from Stanford, was a well-known and long-term justice of the peace in San José. He and his wife Mabel Allen, daughter of progressive orchardist Lester Allen, lived here with their son John. Upon his death in 1966, the Urban A. Sontheimer Award was established at Stanford for the student receiving the second-highest grade point average at the end of his or her third Stanford year.

ABOVE: The Sontheimer house in Palm Haven.

BELOW RIGHT: The St. Francis Bungalow Court. Used with permission of SJSU Library Special Collections and Archives.

St. Francis Court Bungalow Court
San José (Demolished)

As the population of San José and Santa Clara County continued to grow, the need for multi-unit dwellings increased. Starting in 1920, commissions for apartment buildings, duplexes, and single-to-multi-family residential conversions doubled for Wolfe & Higgins.

BELOW: The chimney on the Teixeira house is decorated with terracotta escutcheons.

BOTTOM: The Teixeira porch has the round front steps seen on so many Wolfe & Higgins houses, as well as a triple–arched entrance supported by twisted columns with acanthus leaf capitals.

The bungalow court was one new type of multi-unit complex that had started to become very popular in the 1920s. A bungalow court typically consisted of six to ten small houses placed in a U-shape around a common yard. Pasadena architect Sylvanus Marston designed the first bungalow court in Southern California in 1909, and they grew increasingly popular, particularly in California, providing affordable living and a community atmosphere. Spanish Revival became the most common architectural style for bungalow courts. By the mid-1920s, the *Pacific Ready-Cut Homes Catalog* offered plans for several Spanish Revival bungalow courts.

St. Francis Court, a ten-unit complex commissioned by insurance agent and real estate developer Matthew Glennon, was the first bungalow court Wolfe & Higgins designed. Coincidentally—or maybe not—it had the same name as Sylvanus Marston's first bungalow court in Pasadena—St. Francis Court. Unfortunately, Wolfe & Higgins's St. Francis Court has been demolished.

Mary and Antone Teixeira House
Santa Clara

This Spanish Revival house was designed for cannery worker Antone and Mary Teixeira, who had arrived from Portugal to Santa Clara in 1912.

Annie and Hiram Tuttle House
San José

San José attorney Hiram Daniel Tuttle (1856-1928) was still a very well-known attorney at the age of sixty-seven when he commissioned this Wolfe & Higgins house for himself, wife Annie, and their fifteen-year-old son Hiram Jr. The accomplished Tuttle had been the district attorney of Monterey County from 1886-1889, and a judge in the superior court during the years 1903-1904. He was president of the Bank of San José and on the board of directors of the First National Bank, as well as trustee of the San Jose Normal School (today San José State University).

ABOVE: The Tuttle house combines interesting features in a small cottage: eyebrow portico rising above the roof line, overhanging eaves, full-height windows, and oversized decorative chimney. The Palladian arch form in the front entrance was used on several houses by Wolfe & Higgins around this time.

ABOVE RIGHT: Hiram Tuttle had previously lived in this much larger house designed by Wolfe & McKenzie in 1901.

RIGHT: Hanchett Park house designed for Eve Wills.

Eve Wills House
San José

This house designed for Eve Wills, bookkeeper at the *San Jose Mercury Herald*, has a tiled hipped roof and a covered porch with a tiled arched roof. Triple-arched front windows, low walls with contrasting caps, a curvilinear wing wall, and decorative cartouches add to the appeal of this Hanchett Park home.

Faye and Carl Wolfe House
San José

Carl Wolfe and his wife Faye lived in a number of houses in and around the Palm Haven neighborhood, and Carl built speculative houses there as well. This Spanish Revival house with arched wing wall leading to the garden is one the couple lived in from 1923-1924.

RIGHT: 1923 Palm Haven house for Carl and Faye Wolfe.

BELOW: Matching garages were standard for Wolfe & Higgins. The Wolfes' garage is attached to the house by means of the arched wing wall.

BOTTOM: Alma and Clarence Wolff house.

Alma and Clarence Wolff House
San José

This house, built in Hanchett Park for cannery sales manager Clarence Wolff and his wife Alma, has many of Wolfe & Higgins's favorite features: jerkinhead roof, sets of triple-arched windows with twisted spiral mullions, an arched front entrance, and a facade adorned with cartouches and scrollwork. The small upper balcony with fluted corbel shaped like a stoup (baptismal font) and curved iron railing appears on many Wolfe & Higgins buildings. False shutters with cutouts, something that became a regular element on Wolfe & Higgins houses, are seen on the small upper window.

1924

1n 1924, Wolfe & Higgins worked on about fifty projects, a mix of residential and commercial buildings. Notable works this year included the Corte de Flores bungalow court of San José (see page 113) and the Venetian Court complex of Capitola shown on page 122.

Esther and Warren Allen House
Stanford

This one-and-a-half story Tudor Revival house on the Stanford campus was designed for Warren Dwight Allen, the Stanford University organist who later became the university's dean of music. The original plans show that Allen had a built-in music case; it was rumored that an arched nook was also built to accommodate an organ.

An exterior arch leads into a walled courtyard with an original tiled fountain. Inside, the living room features a high vaulted ceiling with exposed beams. On the exterior front wall is a huge focal window with multi-paned sidelights and a large center pane. On the opposite end of the living room, a high arch with turned balusters adds a decorative element to the room, echoing the repeated arches within the house and creating a visual reference to organ pipes.

Warren and Esther Allen owned the house from 1924 until 1955. Allen was an accomplished self-starter; at the time he began working at Stanford in 1918, he had no college degree. In 1934, he earned a BA from Stanford, following it the next year with a master's degree at the University of California at Berkeley, a PhD from Columbia in 1939, and a MusD from the College of Pacific in 1941.

BELOW: A Beaux Arts–style bracket supports the ceiling beam in the Allen living room.

BOTTOM LEFT: Front window in the Allen living room.

BOTTOM RIGHT: The arched nook in the living room was rumored to have been originally designed to hold an organ.

The Moroccan lamp was installed by original owner Warren Allen.

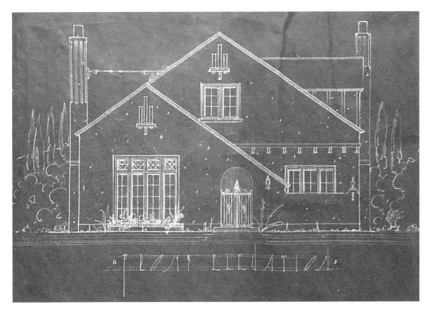

ABOVE: Tiled fountain in the Allen house courtyard.

TOP: Warren and Esther Allen's house at Stanford.

ABOVE: The original blueprint for the Allen house went through several iterations before finalizing. This plan shows a chimney on the right that eventually was moved to the back.

Ernestine and Rene Brassy House
San Francisco

This elegant Italian Renaissance Revival house with tile roof and exposed rafter tails, Tuscan pillars supporting the triple-arched main entrance, and decorative keystones in the arched first-story windows, was commissioned by Rene Brassy and his wife Ernestine in the Balboa Terrace neighborhood of San Francisco.

Rene Brassy, born in 1876, was the wealthy heir of Ferdinand Brassy, who had been a vintner, bank president, and owner of the Brassy & Company mercantile business in San José. Rene Brassy worked for his father's business, moving back and forth between Los Angeles, Long Beach, and San José. The Brassys returned permanently to the Bay Area in 1924 where Rene began selling real estate. The Brassys lived in the Balboa Terrace house for less than two years, then hired Wolfe & Higgins to design another house for them in Atherton.

RIGHT: The Brassys' home in Balboa Terrace in San Francisco.

BELOW: The side view of the Brassy house shows its oversized decorative chimney, full-height arched windows with ornamental keystones, and second-floor sleeping porch with arched openings.

THIS PAGE: Decorative tile, terracotta trim, and a verdant courtyard are part of the charm of the Corte de Flores.

Corte de Flores Bungalow Court (Marie and Vernon Bemis)

San José

In 1924, Wolfe & Higgins were commissioned to design their second bungalow court in San José for service station owner Vernon L. Bemis. Called the Corte de Flores, the complex, still in use today, consists of seven small flat-roofed houses arranged around a lushly planted court-yard. Vernon and his wife Marie and Vernon's parents Abraham and Mabel lived at and managed the Corte de Flores for many years after it was built.

RIGHT: The Frost house.

BELOW CENTER RIGHT: The Kneeshaw house has a jerkinhead roof and a Colonial Revival porch.

BOTTOM: Michael Madden's house in San José, the last known example of a Wolfe & Higgins design using hollow tile, features gabled roofs and overhanging eaves with dentil molding and decorative keystones on arched windows.

Maude and William Frost House
San José

This Palm Haven house was designed for William R. Frost, secretary of the Guaranty Building and Loan Association.

Marie and Dr. Stanley Kneeshaw House
San José

Respected local physician Dr. Stanley R. Kneeshaw and wife Marie lived in this house in the Hanchett Park neighborhood in San José.

Michael Madden House
San José

This hollow-tile house on the North Side of San José was designed for seventy-year-old Michael B. Madden. Madden, originally from Ireland in 1872, moved to San José after a divorce. He had lived in Rhode Island with his wife and children before moving to San José.

ABOVE: Semicircular steps, decorative chimneys, multiple entries, and ornamental door surrounds are among the Wolfe & Higgins features found on the preserved and restored Mlrassou house.

Justine and Peter Mirassou House
San José

This one-story Spanish Revival home stands on the grounds of what was the Mirassou Winery in the Evergreen section of San José. The Mirassou family founded wine-making and prune-farming in the Santa Clara Valley.

The house was designed for Justine and Peter L. Mirassou. Peter was the grandson of Pierre Pellier, who came to San José in 1853 to help his brother Louis with his nursery in San José. The following year, Pierre returned to France to gather fruits and plants that would grow well in the Santa Clara Valley. He came back to San José with cuttings for pears, apples, plums, grapes, and prunes along with a new wife named Henrietta.

The prune became perhaps the most important fruit grown in the Santa Clara Valley, and Pierre's grapes became the source of the Valley's first wine-making business. Pierre and Henrietta had a daughter, also named Henrietta, who married Pierre Mirassou, a neighboring vintner, and the two families combined to launch a wine-making dynasty. The Mirassous' children Peter, Herman, and John continued the family business, as did the generation that followed them.

In 2003, the Mirassou name was sold to Gallo, and in 2005, the farmland was sold for residential development. The Wolfe & Higgins-designed house as well as the historic Mirassou Winery building were preserved.

Margaret and William Pengilly House
San José

This home in the Hanchett Park neighborhood of San José, built for department store clerk William Pengilly, has an elaborate door surround with Churrigueresque detailing and an ornate focal window with recessed arch. Pengilly worked at the White House, a men's clothing store owned by developer Tony Maderis, who was one of Wolfe & Higgins's biggest clients.

ABOVE: The Pengilly home is an example of Wolfe & Higgins's ability to use varying roof heights, a dramatic focal window, and ornamentation to make the most of a small house.

RIGHT: Closeup of the Churrigueresque door surround on the Pengilly house.

BELOW LEFT: This Wolfe & Higgins tile-roofed commercial building was built for Thomas Pollard in 1929 and used as a Safeway grocery store for many years before it was demolished.

BELOW RIGHT: The Pollards first hired Wolfe & Higgins to design this house with triple arches and quatrefoil upper window.

Lena and Thomas Pollard House and Store
San José (Demolished)

Orchardist Thomas Pollard and his wife Lena had this Spanish Revival house built right off The Alameda in San José in 1924. Five years later, Thomas would have Wolfe & Higgins design a store on The Alameda in front of their house, used as a Safeway grocery store until 1940. Thomas died in 1934 and Lena and their children continued to live in the house. Both the house and the commercial building have been demolished.

Lolita and Dr. Louis Rose House
San José

This distinctive Spanish Eclectic house was built for Dr. Louis Max Rose and his wife Lolita in the Alameda Park neighborhood in San José, a neighborhood that still contains many Wolfe & Higgins-designed houses.

The house is a lively mixture of familiar Wolfe & Higgins elements. Semicircular steps are set at an angle leading up to the open front porch, where a small curved wing wall frames the entrance. An arched front door, segmented to echo the shape of the front focal window, is set under a tiled gable roof. The house has a very long entry hall, atypical for Wolfe & Higgins, behind three round arched windows. Inside the house,

BELOW: Dr. Louis Rose and his new wife Lolita had this house designed to honor Lolita's Spanish heritage.

a set of three round arches supported by Tuscan columns separates the living room and dining room.

Louis Rose was born in Poland (his family name was originally Rosenzweig) in 1882 and immigrated to the United States in 1903. He lived in Chicago and New York, where he was naturalized in 1913, before moving to California, where he practiced medicine in Santa Clara. In 1918, he enlisted in the war and served as a lieutenant in the medical corps. In 1919, Louis married teacher Rose Kohner and they had two children. Rose Rose died in 1922 at the age of thirty-nine.

Rose married Lolita Roca, daughter of Santa Clara doctor Ramon Roca, in 1924. Upon their marriage, the Roses had the home built in the new Alameda Park neighborhood. It was said that the style of the house was chosen because of Lolita's Spanish heritage—her father was originally from Barcelona.

RIGHT: The long entry hall of the Rose home has two different type of arch shapes—the segmented arch of the front door and its sidelights and the round arches of the windows.

BELOW LEFT: Tile detail of the living room fireplace.

BELOW RIGHT: The high central arch, flanked by two smaller arches and supported by Tuscan or twisted columns, is a common exterior element in Wolfe & Higgins houses. In the Rose house, it is used inside, to separate the living room and dining room.

TOP: The Rose house's living room has a barrel-vaulted ceiling and central fireplace.

ABOVE: A Moroccan-style lamp hangs in front of one of the corner built-in living room cabinets.

RIGHT: Fountain in the front yard.

ABOVE: The Tormey house with its many gables.

RIGHT: The arched front entrance leads into a small tiled entry hall. French doors and windows with Mission-style panes are repeated throughout the interior.

Katherine and Mary Tormey House
San José

This Tudor Revival house was built in the Naglee Park neighborhood of San José for sisters Katherine and Mary Tormey, daughters of landowner and farmer James Tormey. The Tormey sisters' brother Thomas lived nearby in a 1904 house designed by Wolfe & McKenzie. (See page 75.)

RIGHT: The living room in the Tormey house.

BELOW: Pocket doors lead to the dining room.

BOTTOM LEFT AND RIGHT: Fireplace and tile detail in the Tormey house. The fireplace tile was made by the California Art Tile Company of Richmond, one of the premier California tilemakers in the 1920s.

Venetian Court (Roth Realty Co.)
Capitola

National Register of Historic Places

The Venetian Court complex is probably the best known of all of Frank Wolfe's work. Today on the National Register of Historic Places, this colorful beachside resort is the recognizable symbol of the city of Capitola.

In 1924, the firm of Wolfe & Higgins was hired by forty-two-year-old real estate agent Henry R. Roth of San José and builder Homer Langdon of Sunnyvale to design a forty-six-unit "bungalow court" and bathhouse on the beach in Capitola that would resemble the buildings and waterways of Venice. Each bungalow was to have a forty-one-foot sea frontage and

RIGHT: The Venetian Court is the symbol of Capitola.

ABOVE: The plans for the Venetian Court were published in the *Santa Cruz News*.

all interior modern conveniences, with enough variety so each looked different. The complex, far bigger than any other known bungalow court (which typically had seven to ten units) would consist of attached units with common walls, all with stucco exteriors, tiled roofs, and decorative relief work including smiling gargoyles and dolphins. The property was to have walkways and gardens with public access. Owners would each be assessed an equal amount for maintenance and upkeep, which is why the Venetian Court is considered to be the first condominium development in California.

The units sold quickly, even before the first phase of the resort opened in August of 1924. The architects and some of their friends and clients were

ABOVE: The Venetian Court. Although
sharing common decorative elements,
each unit is unique.

among those who bought units at the Venetian Court. Interestingly, the Higginses co-owned their unit with Gertrude Gardiner, owner of the apartment building shown on page 101. The initial outlay of the entire complex was estimated at $150,000. Today, a single unit is valued at millions of dollars.

In 1927, after the first twenty-seven units were built, a storm destroyed the sea wall that the Roth Realty Company had built in 1924. The rebuilding of the sea wall was so costly that Roth did not have funds to finish the remainder of the planned forty-six units.

Sometime after the 1930s, some of the units were absorbed into what is known today as the Capitola Venetian Hotel. The hotel, plus individually owned units, make up what is known today as the National Register Capitola Venetian Historic District.

TOP AND RIGHT: Decorative building tops at Venetian Court. Each unit is painted a different bright color.

ABOVE: This two-story unit, today part of the Capitola Venetian Hotel, was originally owned by Frank and Nellie Wolfe.

1925

By 1925, Wolfe & Higgins had become an extremely busy firm. Records show that they worked on more than sixty projects that year.

Adams Apartments (Charles and Mary Adams)
San Mateo

Wolfe & Higgins designed this San Mateo apartment building for builder Charles Adams, who lived in one of the apartments with his wife Mary and their two sons.

Atlas Stores and Apartments (Jacob Atlas)
San José

This set of commercial buildings with four stores and apartments on The Alameda in San José was built for Jacob Atlas. Still standing today, the building is at the corner of Atlas Avenue, which was named for the Atlas family in the 1920s. A scalloped frieze of repeating parabolic arches with acanthus leaf finials, a Churrigueresque entrance, and balconets with relief garlands and wrought-iron brackets are some of the decorative elements that give this building its considerable charm.

Jacob Atlas, born in Russia in 1870, had immigrated to the United States in 1900 and made his way to San José in 1915, where he launched a business as a junk dealer. This soon turned into the Atlas Auto Wrecking Company, and by 1919, Jacob was wealthy enough to purchase a substantial piece of property in downtown San José and start the Atlas Tire Company with offices in both San José and Stockton. With wife Mary, Atlas helped found the Temple Emanu-El in San José.

In addition to the commercial building on The Alameda, Jacob Atlas hired Wolfe & Higgins

ABOVE: Adams Apartments in San Mateo.

BELOW: The Atlas building is at the end of Atlas Avenue, where Jacob Atlas and many of his family members lived.

to work on a number of commercial buildings that are no longer standing. Jacob's oldest son Morris, a real estate salesman in San José, was also a customer of Wolfe & Higgins. Morris Atlas lived in a Wolfe & Higgins house in Hanchett Park built in 1922. In 1928, Morris Atlas commissioned Wolfe & Higgins to design an apartment complex on The Alameda in San José, shown on page 156.

Elizabeth and Clinton Brown House
San José

This house in the Vendome neighborhood of San José was designed for railroad brakeman Clinton Brown and wife Elizabeth.

TOP: Churrigueresque entrance on the Atlas building on The Alameda In San José:

ABOVE: Elizabeth and Clinton Brown house.

RIGHT: Close & Close Goodyear Tire store. Used with permission of SJSU Library Special Collections and Archives.

BELOW: William Close Jr. and his wife Irba lived in this house in the Hanchett Park neighborhood in San José.

Close & Close Tire Store and Service Station
San José (Demolished)

This Goodyear tire distributor in downtown San José was one of many stylish buildings designed by Wolfe & Higgins for the automotive industry. The company was owned by brothers Allen Close and William Close Jr., both of whom lived in Wolfe & Higgins houses in San José.

ABOVE: The Dorr house in the Naglee Park neighborhood of San José has a front courtyard with arched entrance and round steps and false shutters with cutouts.

BELOW: The main wing of the Dudfield house is two stories with an imposing Churrigueresque door surround.

Photograph by Sunny Scott.

Stella and Harvey Dorr House
San José

This Spanish Revival house with front courtyard was built for Lelia Estelle ("Stella") and Harvey E. Dorr. Harvey Dorr was a popular history and social science teacher at San José High School and a Methodist minister. The Dorrs lived in the house until 1937.

Lillian and John Dudfield House
Palo Alto

Lumber company owner John Dudfield and his wife Lillian commissioned this outstanding Spanish Revival residence in Palo Alto in 1925. The Dudfields had previously used Wolfe & McKenzie to design their 1904 Palo Alto house.

John Dudfield of Watsonville had incorporated the Dudfield Lumber Company in 1901 at the age of twenty-eight. The company became the biggest of its kind in the Santa Clara Valley.

ABOVE: The Dudfield house in Palo Alto. *Photograph by Sunny Scott.*

BELOW RIGHT: The Fox house in San Francisco.

The Dudfield house is very similar to the house built in 1922 for the Robert Wrights in San José, with minor variations. (See page 91.)

Hannah and Edward Fox House
San Francisco

Edward E. Fox was a merchant who dealt in metals and scrap in downtown San José and a repeat customer of Wolfe & Higgins, who worked on several of his commercial properties. In 1924, Fox and his wife Hannah moved to San Francisco, where they had Wolfe & Higgins design this two-story Italian Renaissance Revival house in the elegant Presidio Terrace neighborhood.

Mary and George Friend House
San José

This Dutch Colonial Revival house was built in Naglee Park in San José for mine owner George Cox Friend and wife Mary. Friend had lived in Iditarod, Alaska, where he was president of the Dome Creek Branch Mine Owners' and Operators' Association. He moved to Naglee Park in San José in 1915 at age forty-eight and met Mary Pender, a widow with two children. They were married in 1919 and lived in Friend's house until they commissioned the Dutch Colonial Revival from Wolfe & Higgins. This was a style evidently favored by Mary, as she and her first husband David Pender had lived in a Wolfe & McKenzie Dutch Colonial Revival home in the North Willow Glen neighborhood.

The Friend house has some similarities to the house William Higgins designed in 1916 for Dorothy and Wilmer Gross—focal porch with Tuscan columns and gabled vaulted ceiling with exposed beams and dentil molding, front door with a fanlight and sidelights, and tripartite casement windows. The Friend house has a wide single shed dormer, in contrast to the three dormers on the Gross house.

ABOVE: The Dutch Colonial Revival house designed for George and Mary Friend has a surprise on the side—a wrought-iron gate and ornately scrolled corbel.

BELOW: The Friends' house is one of the few Dutch Colonial Revival styles in San José.

Doris and Herbert Grey House
San José

Cannery merchant Herbert E. Grey and wife Doris commissioned this L-shaped Tudor Revival house with brick chimney in downtown San José.

Helmi and Alfred Jones House
San José

Contractor Alfred Jones and his wife Helmi lived in this Dutch Colonial Revival in the Naglee Park neighborhood in San José. Jones was the builder of a number of Wolfe & Higgins houses, including the Tormey house shown on page 121 and the Williams house on page 155. Jones also hired Wolfe & Higgins to design at least one speculative house in Naglee Park.

ABOVE: The Greys' Tudor Revival house.

RIGHT: Alfred and Helmi Jones hired Wolfe & Higgins to design this Dutch Colonial Revival house in Naglee Park.

Clara and Anthony Maderis House

San José City Landmark

One of the most outstanding houses in the Hanchett Residence Park of San José is the home originally built for Anthony "Tony" and Clara Maderis. Real estate developer and entrepreneur Maderis was one of Frank Wolfe's longest and most loyal customers. In 1910, he had hired Wolfe to design a house in Hanchett Park, and he continued to use Wolfe & Higgins throughout the entire lifetime of the firm.

Born in Portugal in 1881, Maderis came to the United States with his parents when he was two years old. As a young man, he worked as a store clerk, and in 1914, he and two partners opened a men's clothing store in downtown San José called the White House. Maderis left the partnership in 1919 and the following year opened another department store in Sunnyvale.

Maderis's primary passion was the development and sale of real estate. Working independently or for the Rucker Real Estate Company, Maderis engaged in thousands of real estate transactions. On June 18, 1922, Maderis opened a new residential development called Alameda Park. Located behind The Alameda in San José, ownership in the tract was a way to live near a prestigious neighborhood at a relatively low cost. Maderis had the land improved with sewers, sidewalks, and utilities, and sold the lots starting at a relatively affordable $775. Owners committed to building a house at a minimum price

RIGHT: Anthony Maderis hired Wolfe & Higgins to convert a one-story house into this two-story showpiece. Today, the house has been meticulously restored and maintained; the owner even bought vintage glass, with its inherent waves, to replace the glass in the windows.

of $3,500. In 1922, this assured respectability if not grandeur; the typical Alameda Park house was a five- or six-room bungalow, Spanish or Tudor or Mission Revival. Two weeks after the residence park's grand opening, seven new homes were already being built.

Many of the new owners in Alameda Park commissioned Wolfe & Higgins to design one-story Spanish Revival bungalows, most likely at the recommendation of Maderis, who was fond of the Spanish Revival style for both his spec houses and his own homes. Spanish Revival accounted

ABOVE: Advertisement for Tony Maderis's Alameda Park, opened in 1922.

BELOW: The current owner of the Maderis house used this historic photograph to ensure that all restorations are authentic to the original.

BELOW RIGHT: The entry hall in the Maderis house.

BOTTOM: Upstairs mezzanine.

for about forty percent of the houses that were built in Alameda Park in the 1920s.

In 1924, Tony and Clara Maderis bought a large property in the Hanchett Residence Park from Annie and Chester Topham. The Topham home was a one-story house built in 1913. Maderis performed major renovations on the house to turn it into a magnificent two-story residence. From the staircase in the entry hall with its lancet windows, to the Churrigueresque entrance, to the full-height arched doors and windows on the first floor, the renovation done for Maderis in 1924 is consistent with other Wolfe & Higgins work of the same period.

In 1926, Maderis sold the house to feed-and-grain merchant Samuel Martin and his wife Lila (interestingly, the Martins had previously owned a Wolfe & McKenzie house they had commissioned in 1907) and soon after moved to the Willow Glen area of San José. Here Maderis developed tracts named after his children, Dorothy and Norval, and had Wolfe & Higgins design still more residences. (See page 178.)

With his love of the Spanish Revival style and his realization that it made a salable and appealing home for the emerging middle class, Maderis is perhaps the person primarily responsible for San José's proliferation of Spanish Revival homes.

ABOVE LEFT: Lancet windows with stained glass panes lead the way up the dramatic staircase in the Maderis house.

ABOVE RIGHT: Tall palm trees frame the staircase tower.

BELOW: Living room in the Maderis house.

RIGHT: Churrigueresque relief work and wrought iron surround the front entrance of the Maderis home.

Marie and William Maxwell House
San José

This house in the North Side of downtown San José was built for automobile mechanic William A. Maxwell and wife Marie. The house is on a raised corner lot, where its ornate chimney and multiple arches with twisted pilasters are shown to best effect.

Alice and Arthur Potter House
San José

When railroad agent Arthur Clifford Potter and his wife Alice had this house built in the Palm Haven Residence Park, it was featured in the *San Jose Mercury Herald* in an article titled "Compact Small Home Combines Conveniences." Frank Wolfe had always been described as the architect to go to if you wanted "something different,"

ABOVE: The Maxwell house.

BELOW RIGHT: The Potter house in Palm Haven.

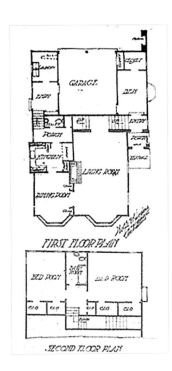

First Floor Plan

Second Floor Plan

ABOVE: The Potter floor plan was published in the *San Jose Mercury Herald*. The author of the article was impressed with the garage built into the house with the bedrooms above.

BELOW: The Raggio house in San José.

and the author of the article seemed to feel the same, opening with, "The feature of being different and individual which is so often lacking in the smaller residence is dominant in...Potter's house."

The cross-gabled house has a projecting front wing with a side-by-side dining room and living room, each with a bay window decorated with cartouches. Among the other decorative elements are wrought-iron balconets, and a covered arched entrance.

"The different floor levels strike one as being a most attractive feature of the house," continued the article. The garage was built into the first floor in the back of the house, a modern design for the times. The garage, which was designed with a laundry area on one side and a den on the other, was accessible through two entrances—from the main entrance hall and from the porch behind the kitchen. Two bedrooms are on the second level over the garage.

Tiny and Peter Raggio House
San José

Wealthy orchardist Peter Raggio and his wife Santina ("Tiny") commissioned this grand house in South San José, with a Churrigueresque hooded door surround with a quoined frame and curvilinear arches over recessed windows. Triple arches are on each of the two flat-roofed side wings.

ABOVE: The Realty Building in downtown San José.

Realty Building (William Atkinson)
San José City Landmark

The ornate Beaux Arts Realty Building in downtown San José was commissioned by real estate mogul William Leroy ("Roy") Atkinson. Atkinson and his wife Charlotte lived in a Frank Wolfe Prairie house that had been designed in 1912 for Atkinson's exclusive residence park, Hawthorne Place.

Roy Atkinson was one of the most successful real estate developers in San José and a very influential man in Santa Clara County. He was the head of the W.L. Atkinson & Company real estate firm and president of the local real estate association. He had been a city council member and head of the San José Chamber of Commerce. His presence as a speaker was in demand at numerous civic organizations.

The Realty Building contained a number of real estate businesses, including Atkinson's, and the Wright-Ely Printing Company on the first floor. Wolfe & Higgins moved their offices into the Realty Building as soon as it was ready.

Margaret and Frederick Roney House
San José

This Spanish Revival house on the North Side of San José was built for electrician Frederick S. Roney and his wife Margaret.

Marie and E.L. Wolfe House
San José

In 1925, E.L. and Marie Wolfe moved from their Spanish Revival bungalow to this multi-gabled Tudor Revival with steep pitched roof and arched door, also in Palm Haven.

ABOVE: Roney house in North San José.

BELOW: The side view of E.L. and Marie Wolfe's Tudor Revival shows the large arched focal window.

RIGHT: The Wolfe house main entrance.

1926

On August 18, 1926, Frank Delos Wolfe died, less than six weeks before his sixty-fourth birthday. He had been working as a builder and architect in San José for thirty-eight years. During that time, he was responsible for well over 1,100 works, both alone and with partners, including eight buildings today on the National Register of Historic Places and countless city landmarks and Structures o f Merit. Throughout his career, he was regularly featured in the *The Architect & Engineer* and *Building and Industrial News* as an innovative designer.

In 1926, Carl Wolfe finally became a partner in the business, and the firm of Wolfe & Higgins continued.

Elise and A. Clyde Alexander House
San José

This two-story Spanish Revival residence in the Rose Garden neighborhood of San José was one of the many homes of A. Clyde and Elise Alexander. Alexander, one of the biggest real estate developers in San José, was a regular customer of Wolfe & Higgins. He earlier hired the architects to design the Venetia Apartments shown on page 89.

ABOVE: The Alexanders built their home in the Rose Garden neighborhood of San José. For decades, A. Clyde Alexander was the developer for many of San José's most desirable neighborhoods.

RIGHT: The Borchers Brothers building.

Borchers Brothers Office
San José City Landmark

Wolfe & Higgins were frequently hired when clients wanted to remodel their houses or commercial buildings to give them a more fashionable Spanish facade. The Borchers Brothers building materials company received a new brick front and some Spanish Revival features.

RIGHT: The Halloran
duplex.

FAR RIGHT: The
Hallorans' home
next to the duplex.

Nina and Philip Halloran Duplex and House
San José

This pair of bungalows was designed for retired builder Philip "P.J."
Halloran in downtown San José. Halloran and his wife Nina, along with
their daughter Amy, a teacher, lived next door to the duplex in a Wolfe &
Higgins-designed house.

Daisie and Thomas Price Houses
San José

TOP: The Price house in the Alameda
Manor Residence Park in San José.

ABOVE: Just a year earlier, the Prices had
commissioned this Tudor Revival house
from Wolfe & Higgins in Naglee Park.

Thomas H. and Daisie Price commissioned this Tudor Revival house in
the new and prestigious Alameda Manor Residence Park. This house was
the Prices' second Tudor Revival by Wolfe & Higgins in as many years—
the previous year, they had a Wolfe & Higgins house built in Naglee
Park.

The Alameda Manor was a small and exclusive development on
Alameda Way, just off The Alameda in San José. Developers Barnett &
Phelps bought the land in 1924 and the following year, presented seven
premium two-story houses, including one announced as the "Home
Electrical," a fully furnished house advertised as being "electrically
equipped throughout with every known time and labor-saving device,
every down-to-the-minute appliance for making the modern home more
convenient and comfortable." The model homes and the Home Electrical
were of the Spanish Revival style, built by the Cook Lumber Company.

Thomas Price was the tiling contractor for the original homes in
Alameda Manor. He and his wife Daisie were originally from Australia
and had come to San José around 1925 from San Francisco, where Price
was active in the Builders' Exchange. The Prices lived their first year
in San José in the Wolfe & Higgins-designed Katie Rogers apartment
building. (See page 105.) In 1925, the Prices had Wolfe & Higgins design
a Tudor Revival house in Naglee Park. By 1928, the family was living in
the Alameda Manor.

Madeline and Maurice Rankin House
Saratoga

In 1926, Maurice and Madeline Rankin moved from their small bungalow in the Hanchett Park neighborhood of San José to a Wolfe & Higgins-designed Monterey-style house in a new subdivision between Los Gatos and Saratoga. Previously known as the Hume Ranch, the location was touted as one of the "show spots of the Santa Clara Valley." In 1921, the James A. Clayton & Co. real estate firm had subdivided 680 acres of the ranch land into large residential and orchard lots.

Monterey is a style derived from Spanish Colonial houses of Northern California. Usually two stories, with a low-pitched gabled roof, these houses are primarily identified by the second-story cantilevered balcony that extends the full width of the house.

The balcony of the handsome Monterey house commissioned by attorney Maurice Rankin and his wife Madeline extends across the back of the house as opposed to the front. The sweeping house with its red tile roof has false shutters—a common feature of the Monterey style and one that Wolfe & Higgins adopted around this time—and it also has a Wolfe & Higgins signature arched entrance with a deep reveal.

Rankin's house was right up the road from a house Wolfe & Higgins had designed the previous year for James Bradley Clayton and his wife Olive. James Bradley Clayton and his brother Willis, a banker, were heirs to the James A. Clayton & Co. real estate firm founded by their grandfather in

RIGHT: The back view of the Rankin house shows the cantilevered full-width Monterey style balcony.

TOP: The Rankin house.

ABOVE: The photograph of the Clayton house that appeared in the *San Jose Mercury Herald*. The Clayton house was designed in 1925, shortly before the Rankin residence.

1850. The biggest real estate firm in Santa Clara County, the company was headed by the influential Frazier O. Reed, owner of a Frank Wolfe house in the Naglee Park neighborhood of San José and grandson of James Frazier Reed of the Donner-Reed Party. The Claytons, as the ones responsible for subdividing the property, had acquired a prime spot in the subdivision. Set far back from the road on secluded acreage, the house, still standing, is not visible from the street Like the Rankin house, the Clayton's house has a Monterey-style upper deck. The Clayton house was featured in the *San Jose Mercury Herald*, in a 1926 article, which said that the house

> ...is so much in keeping with California sentiment and atmosphere that one is attracted by it immediately. Early California Spanish lines have been followed conscientiously, and the rough-troweled whitewashed stucco walls, rough re-sawn timbers and red clay tile roof provide a near-perfect medium to carry out the effect.

May and Dr. James Tebbetts House
Hollister

This Italian Renaissance Revival house in Hollister was designed for prominent Hollister physician James H. Tebbetts and his wife May. The 1926 house has many signature Wolfe & Higgins features: a porch with

Tuscan pillars and a triangular pediment, and arched windows with a pair of twisted columns between the windows. One interesting variation on a feature Wolfe had used in the past is an arched nook in the front of the house, framed by a decorative trellis. (Wolfe had used trellises as decorative elements in the early 1910s.)

The Tebbettses had commissioned Frank Wolfe ten years earlier to design their previous house in Hollister, one of the first known Spanish Revival houses by Wolfe, with its tiled hipped roof and arcaded front porch. It was the first instance of the triple arches separated by Tuscan pillars that was used, in different varia-

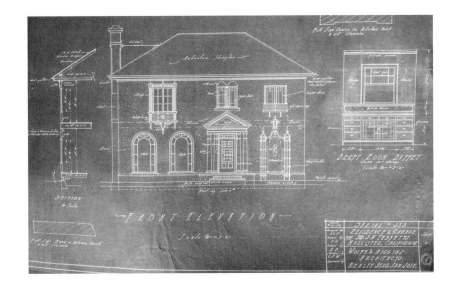

TOP LEFT: The first house May and James Tebbetts had built together was this Shingle-style 1905 combination residence and medical office in Hollister. This building may have been designed by Wolfe & McKenzie, who had already become known in town for their work on the Wapple house in 1908, shown on page 82.

TOP RIGHT: Blueprint of the 1926 Tebbetts house.

ABOVE LEFT: This Hollister Craftsman home was designed by Frank Wolfe in 1911 for Irma and Richard Hardin. Richard was the brother of May Tebbetts.

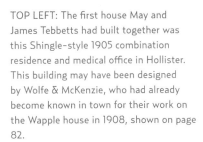

ABOVE RIGHT: Living room in the Tebbetts house.

tions, on perhaps hundreds of buildings over the lifetime of the firm of Wolfe & Higgins. The 1916 Tebbetts house was featured in the *San Jose Mercury Herald* in 1921 as an example of a beautiful and unusual house in the flourishing city of Hollister.

The Tebbettses were familiar with the work of Frank Wolfe when they hired him in 1916. May's brother, Richard O. Hardin, had used Wolfe as the architect for his 1911 Craftsman house, and it is possible that the Tebbettses' first house in 1905 was the work of Wolfe & McKenzie.

Faye and Carl Wolfe House
San José

This Spanish Colonial house built in Palm Haven in 1926 was the home of Faye and Carl Wolfe for about two years until 1928. Like his father and uncle, Carl Wolfe was an active speculator, designing and sometimes building houses, selling them or living in them for a short time. The three houses shown on this page were all places Carl and Fay Wolfe used as their listed address between 1925 and 1930, after which they bought orchard land on the outskirts of San José.

These houses give a sense of the evolution of Carl's design as he moves away from Churrigueresque decor and toward simpler elements such as timbered window headers. This unadorned form of Spanish Colonial house with the tiled shed roof over a broad porch with supporting columns was used with some regularity in the later years of the firm's existence.

TOP: Carl Wolfe's Spanish Colonial house in Palm Haven. The Wolfes lived here from 1926-1928.

ABOVE: The Wolfes lived in this house on the edge of the Palm Haven neighborhood from 1924-1926.

RIGHT: A 1929 Carl Wolfe house in North Willow Glen. He and Faye lived here for about a year.

Carl Jay Wolfe &
William Ernest Higgins

1927-1931

1927

In 1927, Carl Wolfe and William Higgins are on record as having worked on at least thirty projects, about two-thirds of them residential.

Louise and Frank Cox Jr. House
San José

This Tudor Revival with small shed dormer with triple windows built into a steep roof was designed for plumber Frank Cox Jr. and his wife Louise and built in the Rose Garden section of San José.

Edith and Joseph Goldeen House
San José

One of the most distinctive Spanish Eclectic houses on The Alameda in San José was the home of Edith and Joseph Goldeen, owners of the

ABOVE: The Cox house.

BELOW: The Goldeens' house in San José was originally designed for Tony Maderis.

BELOW: Many different types of arches comprise the Goldeen house. The focal window with its graceful curvilinear arch beneath scallops faces the street.

BELOW CENTER: The main entrance of the Goldeen house is a round arch within a pointed arch.

ABOVE: The Gottenberg duplex is on a corner lot, with each entrance on a different street.

Goldeen Furniture store in downtown San José. The Goldeens were both originally from Russia; Joseph had come to the United States in 1905 at the age of twenty-three and went into the furniture business right away; Edith had been in the country since she was seven years old. The couple lived in Oregon and Montana before moving in 1921 to San José, where Joseph worked as an auctioneer and a dealer in used goods, parlaying his business into a large and successful store in downtown San José at which he sold both used and new furniture.

The Goldeens' house on The Alameda was originally commissioned from Wolfe & Higgins by Tony Maderis, who told his wife Clara that this was to be her house. Reportedly, the Goldeens made him an offer he could not refuse and they took ownership of the house less than two years after Maderis had it built. (This was not the first time Maderis had done this to his wife! The Martins had also made him an offer he said he could not refuse on the Maderis home in Hanchett Park shown on page 132.)

Reflective of Maderis's tastes, the building incorporates a great number of Wolfe & Higgins Spanish Revival features. The cross-gabled house features a front wing with an enormous focal window with a curvilinear arch and a deep reveal. A scalloped frieze extends across the wall under the eave and above the window. The other large windows echo the pointed arch shape.

The front wing, with its many arches, is joined to the very angular two-story back wing by a large, central round turret that houses the staircase, similar to that in the 1925 Maderis house in Hanchett Park. The turret has a narrow window with leaded-glass panes and terracotta screens, and a row of small square vents at the top. The back wing includes a Monterey-style porch on the second floor.

Mabel and Emmett Gottenberg Duplex
San José

This Spanish Revival duplex was built as a residential investment property for CPA and attorney Emmett Gottenberg and his wife Mabel. Today, the building is used as offices.

Salvador LiCursi Apartments and Storefront
San José

This elaborate downtown building with its two-story-high Churrigueresque door surround and lavish ornamental detailing was owned by barber Salvador LiCursi. LiCursi ran his barbershop business on the first floor and rented out the upper-floor apartments. The LiCursi building is still used as a barber shop, with the LiCursi name still on the storefront today.

Bluma and Joseph Polissar
House and Retail Building, San José

Joseph Polissar was a dry goods merchant in San José who had emigrated from Rumania in 1921. Wolfe & Higgins designed this Spanish Revival house for Joseph, his wife Bluma, and daughter Missa. Today used as a law office, the building has retained its square entry tower and curvilinear arched windows.

Joseph Polissar's dry goods store was right next to the house, in a four-store commercial building also designed by Wolfe & Higgins the same year. The building, still standing, is made of reinforced concrete blocks, with dentil molding, rosettes, and decorative columns.

ABOVE: The LiCursi building today.

RIGHT: The Polissar house, today a law office.

FAR RIGHT: Joseph Polissar's four-store building was designed by Wolfe & Higgins the same year as the house.

Sacred Heart Convent

Hollister

In 1927, Wolfe & Higgins designed a convent school and dormitory in Hollister, to replace the existing Sacred Heart Parish School that had been started in 1891 by four nuns of the Sisters of Charity to help families in need. According to the March 11, 1927 edition of the *Hollister Advance*, the school was to be "of the most modern type" with modern lighting, ventilation, and heating.

The school was a combination grammar and high school, built with reinforced concrete, two stories high, with fourteen rooms,

including assembly hall. The dormitory, a Spanish Revival stucco building of three stories with thirty rooms, was home for the nuns. Ground was broken March 27, 1927 and the work was completed by Thanksgiving of the same year.

Plans for Sacred Heart were originally prepared in 1925 by the architectural firm of Shea & Shea in San Francisco, a firm that had already done work in Hollister. For unknown reasons (maybe the cost; Shea & Shea estimated $140,000 for the project), Sacred Heart asked for new bids in February of 1927. The project was given to Wolfe & Higgins, who gave an estimate of $65,000 for the two buildings. The buildings were funded by raising money from local prominent Catholics.

The Sacred Heart Parish School still exists today, celebrating more than 125 years. In the 1930s, the Sisters of Charity were replaced by the Sisters of Saint Mary of Namur, from Texas, and in the 1960s, the Dominican Sisters of Adrian took over management. Since the 1990s, the school has been run by lay-persons and the original convent building is today the Sacred Heart Pastoral Center.

ABOVE: The Sacred Heart Convent is the Pastoral Center today. Part of the original school still exists as well, seen to the right of the Pastoral Center.

LEFT: The entry hall is framed by arches supported by ornate carved corbels.

TOP RIGHT: Second-floor radius balcony with wrought-iron grille.

ABOVE RIGHT: This second-story window has an elaborate low-relief sur-round and a spindled rail balconet.

RIGHT AND FAR RIGHT: Interior details in the Sacred Heart Pastoral Center.

Marian Silva Duplex
San José

This house is another example of a Wolfe & Higgins duplex that appears to be a single-family residence, while giving the residents the sense of having two distinctly different homes. One entrance is a front gable with an arch, and the other is under the overhang of the steeply pitched roof, flanked by decorative brackets and narrow windows that echo the shape of the house's slatted attic vents. The Silva house is the last known example of a clipped roof on a Wolfe & Higgins building.

RIGHT: Wolfe & Higgins designed about a dozen duplexes during the lifetime of the firm. The Silva house in Palm Haven is one example of a duplex that gives the appearance of a single–family residence.

BELOW: The Christopher and Mary Smith house has double gables and an offset front door, as do many of the Wolfe & Higgins Tudor Revival homes.

Mary and Christopher Smith House
San José

Christopher H. Smith was co-owner of the Smith Brothers Auto Trimmers in downtown San José at the time he and his wife Mary had this two-story Tudor Revival house with asymmetrical front entrance built in San José's Naglee Park.

ABOVE: The Williams house.

Mildred and John Williams Jr. House

San José

This handsome Spanish Revival house in the Willow Glen neighborhood of San José was built for John S. Williams Jr. and his wife Mildred. Williams was a manager at the family clothing store, J.S. Williams, founded by his father in downtown San José. The Williams family home where John Jr. had grown up was a Wolfe & McKenzie house. Williams's father, John Sr., had also previously used Frank Wolfe to do architectural work on the clothing store.

Distinctive features on the Williams home are the enormous round arched focal window with rope trim and the high square entrance tower. The house's entrance opens to the side, shielded by a curving wing wall. At the top of the tower are sets of triple open arches separated by twisted columns; the front is punctuated by a vertical row of three oculi covered with wrought-iron grillework. The chimney on the Williams house has its own open arched vents and pitched tile roof. The builder was Alfred Jones, a favorite Wolfe & Higgins contractor and customer. (See page 131.)

1928

In 1928, Wolfe & Higgins completed some of their most memorable residential designs, with large homes commissioned by some of the most powerful people in San José.

Atlas Apartments (Morris Atlas)
San José

This complex consisting of forty apartments was commissioned by real estate salesman Morris Atlas, son of developer Jacob Atlas of Atlas Auto Wrecking. Morris Atlas and his wife Elsie lived in Hanchett Park in a Wolfe & Higgins house designed in 1922.

The apartments, built on The Alameda in San José, were noted for their amenities—a garage for each apartment, a swimming pool, and a putting green. Like the Blanchard duplex shown on page 69, the buildings have external staircases. The buildings and their garages retain most of their original features.

TOP: Morris and Elsie Atlas lived in this Wolfe & Higgins house in Hanchett Park, designed in 1922.

ABOVE: The Atlas Apartments.

Mary and Charles Bigley House
San José

One of the most impressive buildings of the Wolfe & Higgins period is the residence built on The Alameda in San José, for political boss Charles Bigley (1888-1946) and his wife Mary. "Boss" Bigley's political organization controlled most of San José's city government and the fire and police departments. Bigley owned a number of businesses, including a liquor distribution, and in 1926, had started San José's first motorized ambulance service. His political sway enabled his businesses to eliminate competition.

In 1938, local newspapers exposed the fact that Bigley received preferential treatment from San José police, and in 1944, a group of citizens formed the Progress Committee to rid the city of the political machine that could allow a Bigley to have so much influence.

Combining some of the features of the Italian Renaissance Revival houses from the early days of the Wolfe & Higgins partnership and perhaps drawing from forms repeatedly used by Frank Wolfe during the Prairie era, the two-story Bigley house has a symmetrical facade with two front-projecting wings and a central front entry. Asymmetry is achieved with differing windows—the left wing has the standard Wolfe & Higgins triple-arched high windows with twisted columns between the arches, and the right wing has a single large arched window with a deep reveal and a triple-window configuration above. The builder was James E. Perkins, a favorite of Wolfe & Higgins and the builder of choice for some of the firm's most influential clients.

The Bigley design was one customers liked. It was a derivation, although bigger, of a much-admired house designed the same year for Fred and Charlotte Wilson (See page 168.) In 1929, oil magnate Fred Cook hired architect Will

THIS PAGE: The entry hall in the Bigley residence features arched doors and windows and a dramatic staircase with wrought-iron railings and the Wolfe & Higgins signature volute.

Toepke of San Francisco to design a house, just two blocks away on The Alameda, that looks so much like the Bigley house, it is hard to believe it is not a Wolfe & Higgins. Why Cook did not hire Wolfe & Higgins to design his house remains unknown.

Today the world headquarters of the Center for Spiritual Enlightenment, the Bigley House retains its original exterior and much of its original interior as well.

ABOVE AND BELOW: Exterior elements at the Bigley residence.

PREVIOUS PAGE SPREAD: The Bigley house.

Louise and William Casey House
San Mateo

Real estate salesman William W. Casey and his wife Louise commissioned this elegant multi-gabled Tudor Revival home in the Baywood neighborhood of San Mateo.

RIGHT: Wolfe & Higgins designed several houses in San Mateo, including this one for the Caseys.

Mission Court Apartments
(Robert Hobson & William Beal)
San José

It's hard to believe from looking at the outside, but the Spanish Revival Mission Court Apartments in the historic Hensley District of San José were built from the 1893 Dougherty Mansion. Lumber magnate William Patrick Dougherty and his wife Anna Fenton Dougherty lived in the house, which took up the entire block, until Anna Dougherty died in 1931. The property passed to Robert "R.O." Hobson, wealthy owner of a mining company and an occasional land developer, and William H. Beal, a real estate broker. The pair hired Wolfe & Higgins to do the renovations that would turn the mansion into a thirty-five-apartment complex that is still today a blend of Victorian and Spanish architecture.

BELOW: The Mission Court Apartments.

Rose and Frank Perry House
San José

Ice cream truck driver Frank Perry, his wife Rose, and their two young children lived in this Spanish Revival house in the Alameda Park tract in San José. The two-bedroom home, with its arched windows, twisted columns, and decorative details, is typical of the architect-designed homes in Alameda Park, the residence park founded by Tony Maderis in 1922.

Wolfe & Higgins provided thirty-six pages of specifications along with the blueprints for the house. Every detail down to nail size, ironwork, vents, grilles, and brickwork, were specified as to the brands and the measurements to the eighth of an inch. The excerpt from the specifications demonstrate not only the quality of the work and materials but also the level of control the architects had over every aspect of the buildings they designed:

> The entire works to be executed of the best materials of their several kinds that can be procured on the market and the workmanship to be performed in the most approved and skillful manner...
>
> Exterior preparation: Cover all sap knots and defects in the woodwork which is to be painted with a good coat of pure alcohol shellac before painting. Putty up all nail holes, cracks and defects after priming. Only the best pure linseed oil, and Carters or Red Seal pure white lead to be used. All exterior woodwork to receive a coat of priming composed of oil and ochre, and then two coats of white lead and oil. Colors selected by Architect. All this work to be primed as soon as put up...All plaster Wainscot to have one coat of Vitrilite enamel tints, colors as selected by Architects.

ABOVE: The Perry house in Alameda Park.

BELOW: Closeup of the twisted columns on the arched windows on the Perry house.

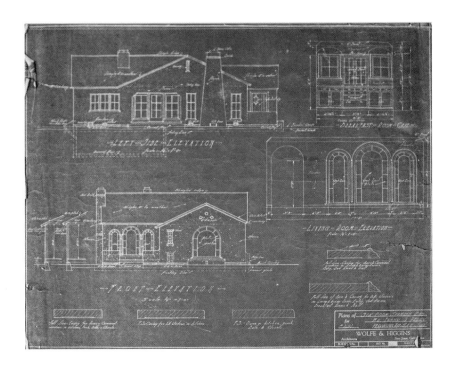

ABOVE LEFT: Blueprints for the Perry house.

ABOVE RIGHT: The breakfast room in the Perry home features built-in cabinets with arched openings.

ABOVE: The central tile on the fireplace was made by the California Art Tile company in Richmond, one of the tile makers specified by Wolfe & Higgins.

RIGHT: The living room in the Perry house has coved ceilings, a wide arched entrance to the dining room, and a ceiling-high central fireplace.

Mava and Woodie Peters House
San José

Woodie J. Peters, principal of the Hester School, and his wife Mava lived in this Spanish Revival bungalow in the Rose Garden neighborhood of San José.

Frances and Gaston Plat Automobile Repair Shop and Residence
San José

This stylish auto repair shop was designed for Gaston Plat to house his business, Plat & Weber, in downtown San José. It features pointed arches, enormous entry arches on three sides, decorative screening, and balconies with wrought-iron brackets and decorative corbels. The residence on the second floor has a projecting window and corner chimney with scalloped bottoms. The service area in back features an arched doorway and Mission Revival-style parapet.

Plat, a mechanic originally from Belgium, lived above the shop with his wife Frances and three children. The building is still used today as a repair shop.

ABOVE: Peters house.

BELOW RIGHT: The Plat building was—and still is—a combination auto repair shop and residence.

BELOW LEFT: The side view of the Plat building shows the residence and attached service area.

Minnie and Amos Williams House

San José

This handsome house in the East Foothills of San José was designed for Amos O. Williams (1876-1953) and his wife Minnie, who lived there with their youngest child Vera and Minnie's mother.

Son of Frank E. Williams, a former sheriff of Santa Clara County, Amos Williams worked for twenty years as a blacksmith in Santa Clara. In 1917, he bought into the Hocking & Williams Undertakers firm in downtown San José. Williams was a popular man, well known for his singing voice (for six years, he was first tenor in the renowned Knickerbocker Quartet in San Francisco) and his striking good looks, something that helped a great deal when he ran for County Coroner in 1918 and became a known political power over the next four terms.

Williams was the coroner in charge during the Brooke Hart kidnapping of 1933, a terrible incident in San José history in which the twenty-two-year-old son of department store owner Leopold Hart was kidnapped and murdered. An angry mob of thousands lynched the suspects in a public action that was condoned and encouraged by officials ranging from the governor on down. Williams held the position of coroner until 1934, when voters, in a reaction to the political machine run by Charles Bigley (page 156) swept the county government of four incumbents, including Williams and Santa Clara County Sheriff William Emig.

BELOW: The Williams house in San José includes notable features such as exposed curvilinear brackets under a tiled hipped roof, an ornate chimney on the front of the house, and a windowed hexagonal wing with tile roof.

Charlotte and Fred Wilson House
San José

This Naglee Park residence was owned by Charlotte and Fred S. Wilson, owner of the Red Star Laundry Company. The house is a forerunner of the Charles Bigley mansion built in the same year. (See page 156.) Today owned by the Roman Catholic Diocese of San José, the Wilson house, with original fixtures, flooring, and layout, survived many years as a frat house and has been painstakingly restored to its original splendor.

The property was originally developed by builder and real estate developer Volney F. Van Dalsem. Van Dalsem came from a family of contractors—his father, Henry Clay Van Dalsem, was a carpenter who had built some of the Wolfe & McKenzie houses—and his brothers Louis and Samuel owned the Van Dalsem Brothers Plumbing, Heating and Sheet Metal Works. In January of 1928, Van Dalsem contracted with Wolfe & Higgins for the design and took out a permit to build the house in Naglee Park. Van Dalsem later commissioned Wolfe & Higgins to design his own home in the Willow Glen neighborhood of San José. (See page 186.)

The Wilson house was featured in the HomeBuilder section of the December 15, 1928 issue of *The San Jose Evening News*. Although the

PREVIOUS PAGE SPREAD: The Wilson house in Naglee Park, today owned by the Roman Catholic Diocese of San José.

BELOW: Living room in Wilson house with its arched windows and high central fireplace

TOP LEFT AND RIGHT: The gracefully curving stair railing and the grand entrance hall in the Wilson house.

RIGHT: The playhouse in the back yard.

article was primarily dedicated to the Wilsons' furnishings, the author did note the layout of the house, the beauty of the staircase, and the fine built-in details. One interesting aspect is the backyard playhouse that was built for the Wilsons' daughters, Jean and Ann, today used as a garden shed. With its portico extending above the line of the hipped roof, it bears some resemblance to Wolfe & Higgins's work. Is it possible that the playhouse was also designed by the architects?

ABOVE: Original back door with arched transom and sidelights.

RIGHT: Dining room in the Wilson house.

1929

In 1929, Wolfe & Higgins worked on twenty-one projects. Very well known and in demand by influential clients, the firm designed several high-profile buildings: the Jefferson Union Elementary School (see page 191), the Cerruti Packard dealership, and the San José Woman's Club.

Lorine and Leland Cerruti
House and Packard Dealership, San José

Only twenty-seven years old in 1929, Leland Cerruti was already a success in the automobile sales and service business. Two years earlier, he had gone into business with Louis Col to form the Col & Cerruti Packard Motor Cars Sales and Service. Louis Col was Cerruti's neighbor and the son of Peter Col, who in 1912 had commissioned Frank Wolfe's best-known Prairie building, the Col House in San José's Hanchett Park. (See page 35.)

In 1929, the partners hired Wolfe & Higgins to design a spectacular showroom for their Packard dealership. The building, still standing today and restored to its original finery, was Wolfe & Higgins's most ambitious realization of the Churrigueresque style they had brought

BELOW: The Cerrutis' Spanish Revival home in the College Park neighborhood in San José.

THIS PAGE: Three stages in the life of Leland Cerruti's Packard showroom. Right, the building shortly after its major restoration in 2009.

RIGHT CENTER: The Packard building before restoration. It's hard to believe that this is the same building.

BOTTOM RIGHT: The original Packard showroom. The cars are visible through the front windows. Used with permission of SJSU Library Special Collections and Archives.

BELOW: The original mica lamps, stenciled beams, stained glass windows, and scalloped edges remain in the interior of the building.

ABOVE: Closeup of the Packard building entrance. The late Michael Casey of San Francisco was the sculptor who recreated all of the original ornamentation. He referred to the photograph shown on page 171 to maintain authenticity.

BELOW: The Bernard Maybeck Packard building in San Francisco, today a British Motors showroom and San Francisco City Landmark. *Photography by Alvis Hendley.*

to San José. The front entrance has an enormous arched fanlight and sculpted surround; the front windows are hooded with sculptural images of Spanish heraldry. Wrought-iron pendant birdcage lanterns hang from the exterior of the building and wrought-iron ornamentation is applied to the fanlight, doors, and an upper recessed circular attic vent.

Packard buildings were well known for their lavish architecture. Southern California in particular was full of ornate Packard dealerships designed by architects such as Morgan, Walls, and Clements, who were masters of the Spanish Revival style. Berkeley architect Bernard Maybeck had designed the San Francisco Packard showroom in 1927 (and been given a Packard Phaeton by the client). That building still stands today, a San Francisco City Landmark.

Wolfe & Higgins worked on several projects connected with Leland Cerruti in 1929. San José political boss Charles Bigley hired Wolfe & Higgins to design a garage (no longer standing) next to the Packard building, which he then leased to Cerruti. And shortly after they worked on the Packard showroom, the architects were commissioned by Leland Cerruti and his wife Lorine to design a two-story Spanish Revival home for them in the College Park neighborhood in San José.

Louis Col withdrew from the partnership and the Packard dealership on The Alameda became Leland Cerruti Inc. Packard Motor Cars. Cerruti ran the business for nearly twenty-five years, after which he continued to work at various jobs in other automobile dealerships.

The San José Packard storefront had been stripped of its ornamentation over the years and looked like a different building in 2009 when the engineering firm Biggs Cardosa bought it. They launched a major renovation, from seismic retrofit to duplication of the original decorative tile, wrought iron, and Churrigueresque sculptured relief work, to return the building to its original condition. Today, fully restored, it is an office building for their company headquarters.

Mary and Charles Kane House
San José

This Tudor Revival house with its very steeply pitched roof was built in the Rose Garden neighborhood of San José for salesman Charles Kane and his wife Mary.

RIGHT: The Kane house has a steep pitched roof sloping down to an open arch that leads to the back.

RIGHT: The San José Woman's Club was completed in 1929 and still function as the Woman's Club today.

San José Woman's Club
San José City Landmark

The San José Woman's Club is one of the best-known works of Wolfe & Higgins. The Woman's Club, still very active today, has been in existence since 1894, when a group of nine women met to form a club in which they would discuss topics of importance. They bought their first building in 1906 and soon outgrew it.

In 1926, the Club announced plans to purchase a new site, and shortly thereafter, selected Wolfe & Higgins for the design work. Spanish Revival was a popular style for many woman's clubs in the state at the time, and Wolfe & Higgins were, of course, well known for their Spanish Revival architecture.

Work was begun on the San José Woman's Club in 1928 and completed in 1929 by contractor Frank Neves of Santa Clara. Neves's own home (demolished) was a Wolfe & Higgins design, and he was the builder of many other Wolfe & Higgins buildings, including the Rose house shown on page 117.

Both the interior and exterior of the Woman's Club contain work by some of the top local artisans of the era. The stun-

ning tiles came from San José's Solon & Schemmel (S&S) Tile Company. S&S did the tile work for many buildings throughout California, perhaps most notably for architect Julia Morgan's Hearst Castle in San Simeon, California.

Landscaping for the Woman's Club was done by Willa Clair Cloys Carmack, one of the few well-known female landscape architects and a writer of articles on gardening and landscape architecture. Cloys, a 1916 graduate of the Berkeley School of Landscape Architecture and the first woman to have received this degree, had also been responsible for the landscaping for Gertrude Gardiner's 1922 apartment building in Stanford. (See page 101.)

OPPOSITE PAGE: Details from inside the Woman's Club ballroom and sitting room.

THIS PAGE: Wrought iron and S&S tiles are highlights of the lobby of the Woman's Club.

1930

In 1930, Wolfe & Higgins worked on thirty-two projects.

Lydia and Anthony Blase House
San José

This large Spanish Revival house with a broad arcaded porch, focal window framed by two curving wing walls, and upper wooden balcony was commissioned in the Willow Glen neighborhood of San José for developer Tony Maderis. Maderis was developing several subdivisions in Willow Glen in 1930, and he used Wolfe & Higgins to design some showcase properties at the entrances to his subdivisions.

Anthony and Lydia Blase bought the house right away and moved in with their daughter Evelyn, living there for the next ten years. Anthony was president of Blase Brothers & Company, a family-owned wholesale fruit company in downtown San José.

BELOW: Blase house, commissioned by perennial Wolfe & Higgins customer Tony Maderis.

Maude and Gus Blockie House
San José

This house designed for Gus and Maude Blockie in the Naglee Park neighborhood of San José is the only known example of a Wolfe & Higgins house designed in the French Eclectic style with a conical roof. When originally built, the house had a wavy false-thatched roof. Gus Blockie was owner of Blockie & Son Furnace and Heating Supplies in downtown San José.

BELOW: The Blockie house, an unusual French Eclectic style with conical tower entrance.

Coincidentally, in the late 1930s, the Blockies' son Raymond and his wife Eleanor, shortly after they were married, moved into a nearby Wolfe & Higgins house—the Spanish Revival one-story house designed in 1925 for Stella and Harvey Dorr. (See page 128.)

Edna and Thomas Callahan House
San José

Thomas J. Callahan was president of the Farnsworth & Callahan Auto Supply store when he and wife Edna commissioned this exceptional Spanish Eclectic house in the Naglee Park neighborhood of San José.

The Callahan house is next door to the Wilson house built in 1928 (page 168). Contractor Volney Van Dalsem originally owned both parcels of land, although he sold the land to the Callahans, who then directly contracted with Wolfe & Higgins, who hired builder Charles F. Keesling. Keesling was responsible for many outstanding Wolfe & Higgins houses, including the Hiller house (see page 85), the Friend House (page 130), the Raggio house (see page 137), and the Cerruti house (see page 170).

The house remains true to its original construction, with both external and internal features preserved. Distinctly different from the more formal and symmetrical Wolfe & Higgins house designed for the Wilsons next door, the Callahans' home is a lively combination of varying roof heights and asymmetrical wings, with a front arched colonnade and large central chimney adorned with decorative tiles. An ornate spiraled grille of wrought iron covers a large oval cutout on the front porch

ABOVE: The chimney on the Callahan house is ringed with decorative tiles.

ABOVE RIGHT: The Callahans' garage was designed to match the house.

RIGHT: The living room in the Callahan house has exposed beams and wide arched entryways.

ABOVE: Wrought-iron lamp fixture.

RIGHT: Fireplace in the Callahan house living room.

PREVIOUS PAGE SPREAD: The Callahan house and spiraled wrought-iron grille on the front porch.

ABOVE: The Clare/DeNegri house.

Rosa and Arthur Clare/Mary DeNegri House
San José

This two-story cross-gabled Spanish Revival house in the Hanchett Residence Park in San José was designed for Arthur and Rosa Clare, probably as an investment property. Arthur Clare, originally from England, had moved to San José from Watsonville where he and his son worked as contractors. The couple did not live in the Hanchett Park house for long, if at all; shortly afterwards, they moved to Santa Barbara.

ABOVE: The high vaulted ceiling in the living room of the Clare/DeNegri house consists of exposed beams and wrought-iron cross supports.

In 1932, Mary DeNegri, a young widow of forty-four and co-owner of the DeNegri, Geoffrey & Origlia Undertaking Company, bought the house when her husband, pharmacist Dismo DeNegri died. Mary lived in the house for more than fifty years until her death in 1984 at the age of ninety-six.

TOP LEFT AND RIGHT: Soaring fireplace in the DeNegri house living room and kiva fireplace in the upstairs bedroom.

RIGHT: Original hexagon arched door with hammered brass hardware is inset in a deep parabolic arch.

FAR RIGHT: The stairway with its filigree wrought-iron railing can be seen through the arched living room entrance.

Hester Dairy (Martin Haas)
San José, Demolished

San José had a number of creameries during the first half of the twentieth century, and Wolfe & Higgins were the architects of many of these buildings, designing three in 1920 alone. The Hester Dairy (now demolished) was on San Carlos Street in San José.

ABOVE: The Hester Dairy. Used with permission of SJSU Library Special Collections and Archives.

BELOW RIGHT: The Van Dalsem house.

Elizabeth and Volney Van Dalsem House
San José

This one-story Spanish Revival house in Willow Glen with trefoil arched entrance was commissioned for and built by real estate developer and contractor Volney Van Dalsem. Van Dalsem was the developer and builder of the Wilson house shown on page 168.

Marie and E.L. Wolfe House
San José

E.L. Wolfe, Frank Wolfe's brother and builder of many of Wolfe's works, built and lived in this two-story house that incorporates many of the style elements Carl Wolfe had introduced during his last years with William Higgins. This was the last house in the neighborhood for E.L. and Marie Wolfe, who had lived in Palm Haven since 1913; they lived here about ten years before moving to Santa Clara.

BELOW: Marie and E.L. Wolfe's last house in Palm Haven.

1931

1931 was the last year for the firm of Wolfe & Higgins. On July 3, 1931, Carl died while working late at night to finish up the plans for the St. Helena Grammar School (page 191). At about three o' clock in the morning, he had an attack of peritonitis and although rushed to the hospital, it was too late to save him. It was said that he had only four hours of work left to be done.

It was a tragic ending for a man who was only forty-three years old, whose skill as an architect was growing every year as he came out from under the shadow of his father.

Neola and Emil Buchser Sr. House
San José

This Spanish Revival house was designed for Emil and Neola Buchser in Willow Glen and built by Robert Herschbach, the founder/developer of the Palm Haven neighborhood. Emil Buchser Sr. was a teacher in Santa Clara who became the principal of the Santa Clara Intermediate School and then superintendent of schools. The Emil Buchser High School in Santa Clara was named after him between 1960 and 1981. Today the Buchser Middle School bears his name.

BELOW: A chimney with its own barrel-tile roof over double rows of open flues and the hexagonal bay are just some of the outstanding features of the Buchser house.

Born to German and Swiss immigrants, Emil Buchser was not permitted to attend school until he could speak English, which finally happened when he was eight years old. Because of his struggle, he did not graduate from high school until he was twenty-three years old. Despite this rocky start, his, and his entire family's, contribution to education was great: Neola Buchser was secretary to the president of San José State and both of the Buchsers' sons became teachers.

Lucia and Dario Della Maggiore Store and Residence

San José

This eclectic building in Willow Glen was a store in front, with roomy living quarters in back for the Della Maggiores and their three children, Their son Sam was raised at this property, and continued to live with his parents after his marriage to Aldina Corbari. Ex-wrestler and public school teacher, Sam Della Maggiore was elected to the Santa Clara County Board of Supervisors in 1952, and is recognized as the first Italian-American to hold that public position.

TOP: Wing wall with arched garden gate at the Della Maggiore house.

ABOVE: Side of the Della Maggiore house.

ABOVE RIGHT: The Della Maggiore house today.

BELOW: The Gladding Brothers office building is built from Petersen-Kartschoke bricks.

Gladding Brothers Office Building

San José

Built as an office for the new Gladding Brothers Manufacturing Company in San José, this is one of the few brick buildings designed by Wolfe & Higgins.

The Gladding Brothers Manufacturing Company was started in 1929 by Augustus and Charles Gladding, sons of the founders of the famous Gladding McBean ceramics company of Lincoln, California. The brothers had bought the Petersen-Kartschoke Brick Company of San José (which manufactured brick, terracotta, sewer pipe, and tile) and used the plant to start manufacturing clay pipes and flues.

Mildred and Herschel Graham House
San José

This house in the Palm Haven neighborhood of San José was the home of Herschel Graham, a manager at the local Woolworth store, and his wife Mildred. The house was originally built by contractor Adolph Goldstein as an investment property. Goldstein built houses all over San José, using Wolfe & Higgins as his architects. (See page 79.)

ABOVE: This Palm Haven home with walled front courtyard and multiple arches was commissioned and built by Adolph Goldstein, one of Wolfe & Higgins's best customers.

RIGHT: Wolfe & Higgins did not limit their work to San José. This house with its broad arcaded porch and decorative brackets under the eaves, was built in Burlingame for contractor E.J. Hargrave.

Mary and Edmond Hargrave House
Burlingame

This Spanish Revival home with arcaded front porch with twisted pillars and ornamental grillework was designed for contractor Edmond "E.J." Hargrave and his wife Mary of Burlingame.

ABOVE: The front entrance compound arch. The *St. Helena Star* called it, "a work of art and a splendid asset to the street."

BELOW: The Jefferson Union Elementary School, no longer standing, was built for the Santa Clara Unified School District and completed in 1929. It so impressed the St. Helena school board that they hired Wolfe & Higgins to design the St. Helena Grammar School.

NEXT PAGE SPREAD: The St. Helena Grammar School today.

St. Helena Grammar School
St. Helena

The final building of the Wolfe & Higgins partnership was one of the most outstanding buildings of the history of the firm, the grammar school in St. Helena, California, in Napa Valley. The ornate Spanish Revival building, with its bell tower with tiled hipped roof and low-relief carving on the arches, columns, windows, and cornices, is not only still standing, but it is still in use as an elementary school and it still retains most of its original character-defining features.

In February of 1931, the St. Helena school board trustees met to establish a bond issue for $112,000 to build a new school to replace the current building. Although only thirty years old, the building had been declared unsafe.

The first architect selected for the job was famed San Francisco architect William Weeks, who had designed schools and Carnegie libraries all over Northern California. In March, Weeks was working on preliminary plans, but before the month ended, Weeks had resigned, or been released, from the job.

The school district hired the architects based on their recent work on the Jefferson Union Elementary School of Santa Clara, which the trustees had visited and greatly admired. The trustees asked Wolfe & Higgins to come close to duplicating the Jefferson Union School, with some improvements, mainly the addition of a nearly full-sized basement to be used for storage and backstage rooms for the auditorium. The initial design was approved and the architects continued to work on plans through July.

On July 3, 1931, while working on the final plans for the St. Helena Grammar School, Carl Wolfe died. William Higgins continued to oversee details of the project until the building was completed in 1932. The final cost of the building was $70,000, a surprisingly low cost even then.

The building was a huge hit when completed. The *St. Helena Star* provided a detailed description of the building, writing the following:

> The building is one of which the community may well be proud. Modern in every respect and beautiful in design, it reflects credit upon the architects Wolfe & Higgins. The main entrance, facing Kearney Street, is a work of art and a splendid asset to the street. Viewed from all angles, the school is pleasing to the eye.

THIS PAGE: Interior details of the auditorium in the St. Helena Grammar School. Wolfe & Higgins designed all the light fixtures expressly for the school. Local artist Carl Hilker did the stencil work and other painting in the auditorium.

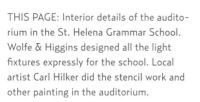

RIGHT: The highly decorative compound arch of the entrance and the high bell tower are the focal points of the St. Helena Grammar School.

BELOW LEFT: The concrete blocks are evident in the arched entrance to the school.

BELOW RIGHT: The bust of assassinated president William McKinley had been unveiled at the old St. Helena Grammar School in 1902, a year after McKinley's funeral, and was kept when the new school was finished in 1932. The bust was sculpted by nationally known sculptor Robert Aitken of San Francisco, most famous for the West Pediment of the United States Supreme Court Building and the Dewey Monument in San Francisco.

Higgins On His Own 1931-1936

After Carl Wolfe's premature death, William Higgins continued to work on his own, completing some of the jobs that Carl Wolfe had started earlier. It was no longer possible to maintain the rapid development for which the firm had been known. The Great Depression, which had begun in 1929, surely affected business, as did the loss of Carl Wolfe as a design partner. In addition, Higgins was aging and may have already been experiencing increasingly poor health. The period from 1932 through the end of 1935 shows records of fourteen projects completed.

Elizabeth and Harold Stern House
San José

One of the more opulent homes in Palm Haven is this house designed for Harold K. Stern, manager at his family's luggage store, F.M. Stern Ltd, in downtown San José. Founded in 1854, the store is still in existence today at a San José mall, with the fifth generation of Sterns running it.

The Stern house is actually a renovation of a single-story home built in 1924. In 1934, William Higgins provided an extensive redesign that added a second floor, bathrooms, and Spanish Revival features such as the upstairs balcony with triple arches and twisted columns, the large arched focal window with deep reveal, and decorative trim.

Master builder James E. Perkins was the contractor on the 1934 renovations. During his career of more than fifty years in the construction business, Perkins was responsible for many of the finest buildings in the area, and was a favorite of Wolfe & Higgins. Among the homes he built for Wolfe & Higgins clients were those for the Jordans (page 63), the Sims (page 65), the Brassys (page 112), the Bigleys (page 156), and the Porters (page 197).

BELOW: The Sterns' house was turned into a two-story Spanish Revival residence in 1934.

Josephine and Dr. Edwin Porter House

San José

This striking two-story Spanish Colonial house with brick veneer near the East Foothills in San José was built for physician Edwin Porter and his wife Josephine, who lived there with their daughter Virginia. The house had been in the planning stage since spring of 1931 while Carl Wolfe was still living, and shows clear signs of Carl's handiwork, with the second-story Monterey porch and the first-floor shed roof over a porch supported by timber posts. Note the tapering chimney and grilles formed from bricks on the chimney and the front of the house. Plans for the Porter house and bids for the work underwent numerous revisions before construction was completed in 1933.

Higgins & Root

William Ernest Higgins died at the age of sixty-four on January 25, 1936. Upon his death, his son William ("Bill") Lewis Higgins (1911-2006), only twenty-four years old, took over the business. Without an architecture license (he was to obtain one ten years later), Bill Higgins took on a business partner, the highly respected architect Chester Root (1905-1977). Root had studied architecture at the University of California, Berkeley.

He received a master's degree from Harvard University in 1930, then worked in New York until 1935 before returning to California to go into business with Higgins. Root became the first architect appointed to the Santa Clara County Planning Commission, and Higgins and Root were founding members of the Santa Clara Valley Chapter of the AIA.

Bill Higgins continued the level of productivity started by his father and Frank Wolfe in 1917. Higgins & Root Associates, AIA became one of the most prolific local architectural firms of its time. The firm continued in business for more than fifty years, designing banks, churches, civic buildings, residences, and more, and was responsible for many schools and structures at local universities and colleges. One of their best-known projects was the *Sunset Magazine* campus in Menlo Park (with Cliff May). The firm won many awards in the 1960s and 1970s. After Root's death in 1977, Higgins partnered with another architectural firm and the business became Higgins & Root Elmore Titus.

Epilogue

The contributions of Frank Delos Wolfe and William Ernest Higgins are all around us today. There are more than 200 documented Wolfe & Higgins buildings still standing today, many of them locally known for their beauty and architectural interest, even when the architect has not been known. And because of the many local developers and builders who saw the value in, and appeal of, the Wolfe & Higgins designs, there are hundreds more houses based on or replicated from Wolfe & Higgins designs, built until well into the 1930s.

The legacy of Frank Delos Wolfe and William Ernest Higgins lives on in their work, a body of work that, thanks to the prolific output of this remarkable firm and their ability to tap into the needs and desires of clients, has helped to create the architectural landscape of the Santa Clara Valley and of San José in particular. The long-lasting value of the work of Wolfe & Higgins cannot be denied; these buildings remain because they are timeless—they are beautiful, they are harmonious, they are as comfortable for today's owners as they were for their original owners. In a time when so many buildings are the victims of the wrecking ball instead of being allowed to grow old gracefully, it often takes a special building to survive.

Appendixes

List of Works

Wolfe & Higgins 1918-1931

This section lists all known Wolfe & Higgins projects designed during the lifetime of the firm. The existing buildings are not open to the public. Please respect the owners' privacy and property when observing these buildings.

Year	City	Address	Project	Owner	Builder	Extant	See
1918	Cupertino		School	Cupertino Union School District		N	
1918	Los Altos	436 University Ave	House	Tooker, Ralph M.		Y	
1918	Los Gatos	135 W Main St	Convert to post office	Rankin, William B.		Y	page 53
1918	Morgan Hill	19665 Hale St	House	Tilton, Howard	Ouimet, Benjamin	Y	
1918	Paicines		House	Renshaw, H.P.		N	
1918	San José	Santa Clara & Fourth St	Garage	Alliance Land Co.	Thomas, Charles W.	N	
1918	San José	28 W Santa Clara St	Commercial remodel	Clayton Real Estate		N	
1918	San José		Stores (3)	Fields, M.		Unk	
1918	San José	Market & St. James St	Apt	Gondolf, N.	Summers, R.O.	N	
1918	San José	19 S First St	Store remodel	Howes, George		Modi-fied	
1918	San José	293 S Second St	Undertakers	Monahan, Thomas		N	
1918	San José	190 S First St	Jewelry Store	Ryder, George		N	
1918	Santa Clara	600 W Santa Clara St	Fuel station	Bisceglia Brothers		N	
1919	Hollister	Fourth St	House	Curtis, Dr. Ralph G.		Unk	
1919	Mountain View	1885 Miramonte Ave	House	Eastwood, Joseph	Jorgensen, Peter	Y	page 61
1919	San José	172 W Santa Clara St	Garage	Atlas, Jacob		N	
1919	San José	59 W Santa Clara St	House alterations	Auzerais Estate	Wolfe, E.L.	N	
1919	San José	550 S First St	Carriage factory	Broedel, Michael	Miller, J.H.	Y	
1919	San José	48 N Third St	Funeral home alterations	Curry & Grippenstraw		N	
1919	San José	184 S Thirteenth St	House	Curtner, Belle & Walter J.	Lindblom, George	Y	page 59
1919	San José	91 S Third St	Apt Bldg alterations	Gilger, Frank B.		N	
1919	San José	345 E San Antonio	Convert to Apts	Hayward, Mrs. Mary	Cunningham, S.B.	N	
1919	San José	1884 The Alameda	House	Jordan, Peter A. & Ida	Perkins, James E.	Y	page 63
1919	San José	399 N Third St	House	Lewis, Nancy B.		N	
1919	San José	Moorpark Ave	House	Luraus, L. H.		N	
1919	San José	32 S Thirteenth	House addition	McCullough, James H. Jr.		Y	
1919	San José	15 N Second St	Lodge	Moose Club	De Smitt, Hector	N	
1919	San José	1299 Yosemite Ave	House	Nelson, Emily & George P.	Dowle, John F.	Y	
1919	San José	495 Stockton St	Addition	Polhemus, Charles B. & E. R.	Wolfe, E.L.	N	
1919	San José	655 S Second St	House	Ryan, George W. & Mary E.	Lindblom, George	N	
1919	San José	622 Morse St	House	Sim, Douglas & Marcella	Perkins, James E.	Y	page 65
1919	San José	44-48 N Market St	Store remodel	Williams, John S.	Moore, W.E.	N	
1919	San José	167 N Fourth St	House	Worcester, Harris C.		N	
1919	Santa Clara	Franklin St & Washington St	Town hall clock	City of Santa Clara		N	
1919	Santa Clara	Franklin St	Warehouse	Parker, Charles	Summers, R.O.	N	

Year	City	Address	Project	Owner	Builder	Extant	See
1919	Santa Clara	Franklin St & Washington St	Store remodel	Scheller, Victor	Morrison Brothers	N	
1919	Sunnyvale	113 S Mary Ave	House	Irvine, Anna		Y	page 62
1920	Campbell	400 E Campbell Ave.	Bank	Curry, Benjamin O.	Field, Z.O.	Y	page 70
1920	Fremont		School heating plant	Centerville School		N	
1920	Fresno	Tulare St & Fulton Mall	Repairs	Forsyth Bldg		N	
1920	Hayward	2451 W Tennyson Rd	House	Oliver, Emilie & Adolph A.		Y	
1920	Mountain View		School additions	Mt. View School District	Minton Co., The	N	
1920	San Francisco	444 Grant Ave	Store	Roth, Henry R., Ellen, Marie & Mary F.	Vukecovich & Bagge	Modified	
1920	San José	(Temporary)	Exposition	100 Per Cent Industrial Exposition		N	
1920	San José	500 S First St	Commercial	Austin, H. Lysle	Nommensen, E.	N	
1920	San José	152 Rhodes Ct	House	Bain, Thomas		Y	
1920	San José	1225 McKendrie St	House	Berggren, Ralph		Y	page 68
1920	San José	Winchester Blvd & Williams Rd	House	Bettinger, T. W.		N	
1920	San José	41-43 Hawthorne Way	Two apts	Blanchard, Dr. Thomas L. & Miriam	Scherrebeck, Thomas	Y	page 69
1920	San José	439 S First St	Auto dealer	Curtner, Walter J. & Wright, Robert	Wolfe, E.L.	Y	page 69
1920	San José	W Santa Clara St	Garage	Graves, John H.	Moore, W.E.	Unk	
1920	San José		School addition	Hawthorne School	Vaughn, M.C.	N	
1920	San José	Race St	School	Lowell School District	Wolfe, E.L.	N	page 67
1920	San José	169 Park Ave	Apt bldg alterations	Mills, M.	Jorgensen, Peter	N	
1920	San José	Saratoga Ave	House	Murdoch, Henry P.	Wolfe, Carl	N	
1920	San José	96 E Santa Clara St	Lodge alterations	Odd Fellows	Field, Z.O.	N	
1920	San José		School	Penetentia school district		N	
1920	San José		Commercial	Royal Tailors		N	
1920	San José	97 N First St	Office alterations	Rucker Co.	Haskins, A.F.	N	
1920	San José	S Second St at Fountain Alley	Commercial alterations	Rucker, James	Thorpe, J.C.	N	
1920	San José	N Seventh St	School addition	San José Horace Mann School	Morrison Brothers	N	page 67
1920	San José	Unk	House	Stutsman, Claude		Unk	
1920	San José	324 Winchester Blvd	House	Thrift, Edgar B.	Nommensen, E.	N	
1920	San José	1024 Ramona Ave	House	Wolfe, Frank D. & E.L.	Wolfe, E.L.	Y	
1920	San José	First St	Alterations	St. James Hotel		N	
1920	San José	Margaret between Sixth & Seventh Sts	School addition	School	Wolfe, E.L.	N	
1920	Santa Clara	Santa Clara (all over town)	Houses (30)	Bank of Italy, Pacific Manufacturing Co., Garden City Bank		Unk	
1920	Santa Clara		Cal Rex Theater alterations	Lion, Ennio		N	
1920	Santa Clara	Washington St	Auto service	Scheller, Victor	Morrison Brothers	N	
1921	Carmel		Cottage addition	Wolfe, Nellie & Frank		Unk	
1921	Fremont		School heating plant	Niles Grammar School		N	
1921	Gilroy	Gilroy	School additions	Madrone School district		N	
1921	Los Altos		Houses (2)	Unk		Unk	
1921	Maxwell		2-story brick hotel	Hardin, George B.		N	
1921	Morgan Hill		School	Burnett School District		N	
1921	Morgan Hill	E side of Gilroy	School	Gates, John		N	

Year	City	Address	Project	Owner	Builder	Extant	See
1921	Mountain View	N/A	Tea House (was not built)	Smith, Victor M.		N	
1921	San José	Pierce Ave.& S Market St	Garage & auto sales bldg	Albertelle & Figone		N	
1921	San José	1572 Hanchett Ave	House	Alexander, A. Clyde	Alexander, A. Clyde	Y	
1921	San José	162-190 W Santa Clara St	Commercial Bldg alterations	Atlas, Jacob		N	
1921	San José	616 Morse St	House	Bassler, Alice		Y	page 71
1921	San José	285 Balbach St	House	Battaglia, John		N	
1921	San José		House	Dinapoli, Peter	Hauser, Carl C.	Unk	
1921	San José	1915 The Alameda	House	Dixon, Hugh & Etta	Wolfe, Carl	N	
1921	San José	1268 Sierra Ave	House	Donovan, Gertrude	Lindblom, George	Y	
1921	San José	273 S Fifteenth St	House	Donovan, Joseph & Ethel	Huxtable, F.J.	Y	page 72
1921	San José	E Empire St	School additions	Grant School, San José School District	Vaughn, M.C.	N	page 67
1921	San José	112 Auzerais Ave	House	Harms, Henry A.		N	
1921	San José	1855 The Alameda	Apt Bldg	Lloyd, Arthur H.		N	
1921	San José	1174 Fremont St	House	Maderis, Anthony W.		Y	
1921	San José	487 N Second St	House	Preston, Harry & Elsie	Maurer, Carl C.	Y	page 73
1921	San José	1158 Fremont St	House	Prussia, Leland & Doris		Y	
1921	San José	1252 S First St	House	Roffinella, John P. & Kohler, Maria W.	Ouimet, Benjamin	N	
1921	San José	1774 Almaden Road	House	Sanfilippo, Gaetano & Anna		N	
1921	San José	584 Coe Ave	Houses (3)	Scaglione, Louis A	Scaglione, Louis A	Y	
1921	San José	195 E Reed	Apt Bldg	Scheller, Victor		N	
1921	San José	St. John St	Store	Slavich & Trapani		N	
1921	San José	494 S Cypress Ave	House	Taormino, Frances & Sal	Perino, Michael	Y	page 73
1921	San José		Apt Bldg	Unk		Unk	
1921	San José	791 S Sixth St	House	Wickland, Anton	Youngquist, S.G.	N	
1921	San José	Lincoln Ave	School	Willow Glen school addition	Keesling, Charles F.	N	
1921	San José	259 Washington	House	Wolfe, E.L.	Wolfe, E.L.	Y	
1921	San José	263 Washington	House	Wolfe, E.L.	Wolfe, E.L.	Y	
1921	San José	925 Plaza	House	Wolfe, Frank D.		Y	page 74
1921	San José	1004 Ramona Ave.	House	Wolfe, Frank D.		Y	
1921	Santa Clara	1795 Lexington Ave.	House	Baker, James T. & Sarah		Y	page 71
1921	Union City	3939 Smith St	House	Harvey, Selma & Fred C.		Y	page 72
1921	Union City		House	Oliver, Andrew		Unk	
1922	Hollister	558 Fifth St	House	Hawkins, Mary	Younger, Charles B.	Y	page 82
1922	Hollister		House	Williamson, G. T.		Unk	
1922	Los Altos	San Antonio Rd	House	Aust, Frank W.	Arnott, E.E.	N	
1922	Los Altos	Boyd Ranch	House	Erskine, W. W. & Erskine, Caro	Thorpe, J.C.	Unk	
1922	Morgan Hill	17500 Depot St.	Granary	Morgan Hill Farmers Union	Gales, John	Y	
1922	Morgan Hill	Spring Hill Rd	House	Peller, Peter & Rose	Gales, John	Unk	
1922	Morgan Hill	95 El Toro Ave.	House	Philbrick, Howard & Grace		Y	page 88
1922	San José	1394 Hanchett	House	Aiello, Joseph (Guiseppi) & Rose		Y	page 77
1922	San José	496 W Santa Clara	Garage	Albertson & Fischer	Kilcourse, Martin E. or Gales, John	N	page 55
1922	San José	20 Hensley St	Venetia Apts	Alexander, A. Clyde		Y	page 89
1922	San José	692 Story Rd	House	Allario, Charles	Gaiotto, John	N	
1922	San José	655 E William St	House	Arnerich, Matthew E. & Clara	Wolfe, E.L.	Y	page 78
1922	San José	589 Chapman St	House	Atkinson, Marion & David K.	Arnott, E.E.	Y	page 78
1922	San José	1281 Martin Ave	House	Atlas, Morris & Elsie	Rasmussen, C.	Y	page 156
1922	San José	Market St. near Santa Clara	Garage & stores	Central Improvement Co.	Byron, D.J.	N	

Year	City	Address	Project	Owner	Builder	Extant	See
1922	San José	15-19 S Third St	Wareouse	Costa Bros		N	
1922	San José	140 S Second St	Commercial	De Carli, Louis C. (De Carli & Son)	Gales, John	N	
1922	San José	San Pedro St	House	Fratangelo, Charles	Oliva, G.P.	N	
1922	San José	1289 Martin Ave	House	Goldstein, Adolph	Goldstein, Adolph	Y	page 79
1922	San José	1340 Sierra Ave	House	Goldstein, Adolph	Goldstein, Adolph	Y	page 79
1922	San José	1694 The Alameda	House	Hall, Grace Spencer	Thorpe, J.C.	Y	page 80
1922	San José	1171 Yosemite Ave	House	Hansen, Theodore A. & Verna	Lindblom, George	Y	page 81
1922	San José	25 S Market St	Union Auto Stage Depot	Hart, Alex; Beatty, James; & Turrel, Gus		N	
1922	San José	1186 Hanchett Ave	House	Hiller, Stanley & Opal	Keesling, Charles F.	Y	page 85
1922	San José	75 Clayton Ave	Duplex	Horwarth, William F.	Osborne, J. W. & Knight, R.C.	Y	
1922	San José	1349 Martin Ave	House	Krohn, J.	Petrie & Furtwrangler	Y	
1922	San José	174 S Second	Store	L.C. De Carli & Son Furniture		N	
1922	San José	362-364 N Sixth St	Houses (2)	Long, J.H.	Alexander, A. Clyde	Y	
1922	San José	475 N First St	House	Lyne, Frederick & Bertha	Petrie & Furtwrangler	Y	page 86
1922	San José	1605 The Alameda	House	Maderis, Anthony W. for Maria Careaga	Maderis, Anthony W.	N	
1922	San José	S Santa Clara near Seventh St	Store	Madsen, Hans H.	Summers, R.O.	N	
1922	San José	509 S Fifteenth St	House	McCoy, Helen	Alexander, A. Clyde	Y	
1922	San José	N First St	Apt Bldg	McHenry, Catherine		N	
1922	San José	264 S Fourteenth St	House	McKenley, Harold D. & Ivy	Huxtable, F.J.	Y	page 87
1922	San José	Market St	Apt Bldg	McKiernan, Joseph M.		N	
1922	San José	161 S Seventeenth St	House	Merchant, Baron P. & Stella	Petrie & Furtwrangler	Y	page 87
1922	San José	955 Plaza Dr	House	Moore, Harriet B.	Arnott, E.E.	Y	page 87
1922	San José	N Second St & E. Julian St	Apt Bldg	Murphy, Mrs. W.M.		N	
1922	San José		House	Noethig, William F.	Waltz, Howard	Unk	
1922	San José	210 W Santa Clara St	Addition	Pascoe, Henry J.	Ouimet, Benjamin	N	
1922	San José			Richmond, Cedric		Unk	
1922	San José	46 S First St	Alterations	Security Savings Bank	Summers, R.O.	Y	
1922	San José	1149 Fremont St	House	Seifert, Claude & Angela	Maderis, Anthony W.	Y	page 88
1922	San José		House convert into Apts	Simpson, G.E.		Unk	
1922	San José	31 N Second St	Garage	Temple, Frank M./Temple & Syer		N	
1922	San José	1820 Park Ave	House	Thompson, Walter	Smith, B.J.	N	
1922	San José	570 Race St	Dehydrating Plant	United States Products Corp. of San José	Summers, R.O. or Anderson, E.	N	
1922	San José	1009 Ramona Ave		Wolfe, Carl		Y	
1922	San José	911 Clintonia Ave	House	Wolfe, E.L.	Wolfe, E.L.	Y	page 90
1922	San José	1024 Emory St	House	Wright, Kate & Robert M.	Petrie & Furtwrangler	Y	page 91
1922	San José	1395 Hanchett Ave	House	Yocum, Eliza	Arnott, E.E.	N	
1922	San José	960 Plaza Dr	House	Yocum, Eliza		Y	
1922	Santa Clara	Franklin St	Commercial	Auzerais, John E.		N	
1922	Santa Clara	1510 Franklin St	Duplex	Ball, Louis & Elsie	Kelly, L.I.	Y	
1922	Santa Clara	Franklin St	Printing Plant	Santa Clara News–Auzerais Estate		N	
1922	Santa Rosa	917 College Ave	House	Hunt, Charles W. & Mary		N	

Year	City	Address	Project	Owner	Builder	Extant	See
1922	Saratoga	14500 Fruitvale Ave	Cottage, solarium, & additions to Library	Odd Fellows Home of Calif	Field, Z.O.	Y	
1922	Sunnyvale	Hollenbeck Ave	House addition	Stelling, Henry G. & Alice		N	
1923	Alviso		School additions	Alviso		N	
1923	Belmont	Belmont Ave	House	Hancom, Arnold J.	Greene, W.P.	Unk	
1923	Campbell	N/A - job given to Addison Whiteside	House	Ainsley, John C.		NA	
1923	Fremont	42800 Caldas Ct	House	Hirsch, Otto N.		N	
1923	Hollister	Orchard Rd	House	Schulze, Herbert A & Pearl		Y	page 105
1923	San José	270 S Market St	Fruit store	Alassa, Frank		N	
1923	San José	Second St & Fountain Alley	House Alterations	Archer, Leo B.		N	
1923	San José	452 E Santa Clara St	Apts	Atkinson, William L.	Bridges, H.A.	N	
1923	San José	Second St	Furniture store	Atlas, Jacob		N	
1923	San José	1495 Lupton Ave	House 1 ½ story	Austin, H. Lysle & Sophie	Latta, G.M.	Y	page 95
1923	San José	503 Park Ave	House	Barcelona, Roselino & Mary	Leone, G.	Y	
1923	San José	1155 Yosemite Ave	House	Berman, Charles N.	Lindblom, George	Y	page 96
1923	San José	441 Park Ave	House	Caporelli, Marcellino	Leone, G.	N	
1923	San José	Almaden Rd	one-story House	Cozzo, S.	Neves, Frank	Unk	
1923	San José	25 S Tenth St	Apt Bldg	De Sando, Michael		Y	page 96
1923	San José	1195 Willow St	House	Dreischmeyer, Frank L. & Caroline		Y	page 97
1923	San José	710 E San Fernando St	Apt Bldg new façade	Focherd, J. & O'Neil, L.		Y	
1923	San José		House & garage	Forehand, Clarence		Unk	
1923	San José	561 E Santa Clara St	Gas station	Foster & Stewart		N	
1923	San José	525 S Fifteenth St	House	Glans, George & Sidney		Y	page 104
1923	San José	160 Park Ave	Bungalow Court (St. Francis Court)	Glennon, Matthew J. & Frances		N	page 106
1923	San José	230 N Eleventh St	Duplex	Gollner, Charles N.		Y	
1923	San José	1147 E Santa Clara St	Store	Graves, Bert W.	Ford, R.E. & Thornberg, J.C.	N	
1923	San José	509 Hoover Ave	House	Gray, William H. & Naomi	Smith, B.J.	Y	
1923	San José	185 E Santa Clara St	Commercial	Hall, Garland B.	Nordeen, J.A.	N	
1923	San José	48 Race St	Commercial Bldg	Hamlin, E.C. & Manchle, John P.	Jorgensen & Cook	Y	
1923	San José	N First St	Garage addition	Hoover, Henry		N	page 56
1923	San José	Almaden Blvd & Park Ave	Apt Bldgs (2)	Kocher Estate		N	
1923	San José	542-544 E San Carlos St	Duplex	Kocher, George	Ouimet, Benjamin	Y	page 104
1923	San José	45 W St. James St	Garage	Letcher, Clarence H.		N	
1923	San José	244 Race St	House	Matich, Peter		N	
1923	San José	858 Clintonia Ave	House	McLean, Maurice A.	Wolfe, Carl	Y	
1923	San José	620 Vine St	House	Mingola, Carlo	Maggio, Vincent	N	
1923	San José	First St & E Julian St	Store remodel	Mise, Charles	Thorp, J.	N	
1923	San José	417 S Eighth St	House	Pascoe, Frank E. & Vera	Ouimet, Benjamin	Y	page 105
1923	San José	459 N Eighth St	House	Pavone, James A. & Jessie	Maggio, Vincent	Y	
1923	San José	1498 Lincoln Ave	House	Pfeffer, Frank M.		Y	
1923	San José	340 E St. James St	Apt Bldg	Rogers, Katie		Y	page 105
1923	San José	43 N Third St	Store	San José Tobacco Co.	Field, Z.O.	N	
1923	San José	1251 Park Ave	House	Shepherd, Ernest D. & Rose	Brown & Rucker	Y	
1923	San José	927 Clintonia Ave	House	Sontheimer, Urban & Mabel (Allen)	Wolfe, E.L.	Y	page 106
1923	San José	65 S Second St	Store alterations	Spencer, Charles M.	Sherburne, Percy	N	

Year	City	Address	Project	Owner	Builder	Extant	See
1923	San José	680 E Santa Clara St	House	Taylor, John	Thorpe, J.C.	N	
1923	San José	682 E Santa Clara St	House	Taylor, John	Thorpe, J.C.	N	
1923	San José	Locust St	School alterations	Trustees College Park School District		N	
1923	San José	711 N First St	House	Tuttle, Hiram D. & Annie	Brown, C.V.	Y	page 108
1923	San José	360 N Third St	Apt Bldg alterations	Vining & Connolly		N	
1923	San José	306-318 W Santa Clara St	Shop & Rooming House	Whitney, John & Mary Whitney Hayward	Sherman, H.R.	N	
1923	San José	1163 Mariposa Ave	House	Wills, Eve M.	Furtwrangler, Walter O.	Y	page 108
1923	San José	184 S First St	Store Alteration	Wilson, E.S.	Jorgensen & Thorny	N	
1923	San José	N First St & Julian St	Rooming House alterations	Wise, S.J.		N	
1923	San José	635 Coe Ave	House	Wolfe, Carl & Faye	Wolfe, E.L.	Y	page 109
1923	San José	935 Clintonia Ave	House	Wolfe, E.L./Sold right away to Brice Sainsbury	Wolfe, E.L.	Y	
1923	San José	1045 Ramona Ave	House	Wolfe, Frank D.		Y	
1923	San José	1275 Yosemite Ave	House	Wolff, Alma & Clarence W.	Furtwrangler, Walter O.	Y	page 109
1923	San José	85 S Market St	Lodge	Woodmen of the World		N	
1923	San José		House	Zannucci, Mr.		Unk	
1923	Santa Clara	675 Washington St	House	Teixeira, Antonio & Mary	Berg, N.O.	Y	page 107
1923	Saratoga		House	Van Vliet, M		Unk	
1923	Stanford	624 Mayfield Ave.	Apt bldg	Gardiner, Gertrude & Nellie	Minton Co., The	Y	page 101
1923	Sunnyvale	North side of San Francisco Hwy near Sunnyvale	House add one story	Kline, Walter		Unk	
1924	Capitola	1500 Wharf Road	Venetian Court	Roth Realty Co.	Baird, J.P. and Meyers, William P.	Y	page 122
1924	Capitola	Wharf Rd	Bath House	Roth Realty Co.		N	
1924	Fremont	Irvington Ave	House	Bracher, Herman F.	Douglass, A.A.	Unk	
1924	Gilroy		Lodge	Order of Redmen		N	
1924	Hayward		School	Mount Eden School District		N	
1924	Los Gatos		House	Fuchs, Karl		Unk	
1924	Monte Sereno	Greenwood Rd & Saratoga Ave	House	Sacks, N.S.	Lindblom, George	N	
1924	San Francisco	445 Darien Way	House	Brassy, Rene & Ernestine	Perkins, James E.	Y	page 112
1924	San José		House	Balocchi, Dr. A.J.		Unk	
1924	San José	560 S Seventh St	Bungalow court	Bemis, Vernon L.	McCrary, George & Sharp, Ralph	Y	page 113
1924	San José	Glen Ridge Terrace Tract	House	Blondin, Fred P.	Larsen, L.P.	Unk	
1924	San José	845 Plaza Dr	House	Bossemeyer, Clyde O.	Collins, Charles S.	Y	
1924	San José	351 Josefa St	House	Corey, Harthley & Elizabeth		Y	
1924	San José	1025 Bird Ave	House	Costello, Edward A. & Theresa	Ouimet, Benjamin	Y	
1924	San José	1747 W Fruitdale Ave	House	Di Fiore, Dominico		N	
1924	San José	1029 Ramona Ave	House	Emig, Louis		Y	
1924	San José	262 W Santa Clara St	Auto parts store	Farnsworth & Callahan		N	
1924	San José	655 Coe Ave	House	Frost, William R. & Maude		Y	page 114
1924	San José		House	Geyer, R.T.	Osborne, J.W. & Knight, R.C.	Unk	
1924	San José	97 S Ninth St	Clinic & office	Kapp, Dr. Michael W.	Sherman, H.R.	N	
1924	San José	210 Clayton Ave	House	Kerins, Wade	Anderson, A.	N	
1924	San José	1251 Yosemite Ave	House	Kneeshaw, Dr. Stanley R. & Marie		Y	page 114
1924	San José	750 S Almaden Rd	Store/Apts	Lawrencella, F.		Y	

Year	City	Address	Project	Owner	Builder	Extant	See
1924	San José	795 N Seventeenth St	House	Madden, Michael B.		Y	page 114
1924	San José	Villa Vista Rd	House	Mancuso, Gabriel	DiCola & Weldon	Unk	
1924	San José	114 E Santa Clara St	Store	Markovitz & Fox	Field, Z.O.	N	
1924	San José	3000 Aborn Rd	House	Mirassou, Peter L. & Justine	Anderson & Dias	Y	page 115
1924	San José	Forest Ave	Hospital addition	O'Connor's Sanitarium		N	
1924	San José	Delmas Ave & San Fernando St	Store	Palermo, Joanna	Nordeen, J.A.	N	
1924	San José	1340 Shasta Ave	House	Pengilly, William & Margaret	Berg, N.O.	Y	page 116
1924	San José	80 N Morrison Ave	House	Pollard, Lena & Thomas	Waltz, Howard	N	page 116
1924	San José	245 N Twenty-fifth St	House	Preston, Edward		N	
1924	San José		House	Radero, Mr. T.		Unk	
1924	San José	Park Ave near Market St	House alterations	Redman, J.	Field, Z.O.	N	
1924	San José	920 Pershing Ave	House	Rose, Dr. Louis M. & Lolita	Neves, Frank	Y	page 117
1924	San José	Ninth St near E Julian St	House	Rossi, L.C.	Rossi, L.C.	Unk	
1924	San José	First & St. John Sts	Commercial alterations	Rucker Co.(Lessees)	Thorpe, J.C.	N	
1924	San José	1250 Fremont St	House	Russell, Edward T.	Youngquist, S.G.	Y	
1924	San José	176-180 S Market St	Store alterations	Scheller, Victor	Summers, R.O.	N	
1924	San José	818 Clintonia St	House	Schulz, Bruno & Mildred	Wolfe, E.L.	Y	
1924	San José	595 S Fifteenth St	House	Tormey, Katherine & Mary		Y	page 121
1924	San José	San Fernando St & Third St	Plant	Unk		N	
1924	San José	N Second St near E Mission St	Houses (2)	Vendome Construction Company	Norman, W.H.	Unk	
1924	San José	335 N Seventeenth St	House	Viso, Giacomo & Francesca	Rossi, L.C.	Y	
1924	San José	26 S Eighth St	Alter house into apts	Wright, Samuel B.	Buck, Amos	Y	
1924	San Mateo	15 Hilltop Rd	House	McGowan, Clara M.	Scroggins, Frederick & Caldwell, Robert	Y	
1924	Stanford	675 Alvarado Way	House	Allen, Warren D.	Osborne, J.W. & Knight, R.C.	Y	page 110
1925	Los Gatos	125 Church St	House	Los Gatos Methodist Church		N	
1925	Morgan Hill	Monterey Rd	House	Liston, Richard F.		Unk	
1925	Palo Alto	625 Hale St	House	Dudfield, John D. & Lillian		Y	page 128
1925	Palo Alto	467 Forest Ave	House	Parkinson, George		N	
1925	Redwood City Emerald Lake Hills	56a Oak Knoll Dr	House	Furtwangler, Walter O.	Smith, Sidney	Unk	
1925	Redwood City Emerald Lake Hills	Oak Knoll Dr	House	West, James	Furtwrangler, Walter O.	Unk	
1925	San Francisco	3934 Washington St	House	Fox, Edward E. & Hannah	Coburn, Ira	Y	page 129
1925	San José		School	Alum Rock School District		N	
1925	San José	19 N Second St	Commercial	Atkinson, William	Sherman, H.R.	Y	page 138
1925	San José	982-998 The Alameda	Stores & Apts	Atlas, Jacob		Y	page 126
1925	San José	296 W Santa Clara St	Commercial	Berggren, Ralph	Megna & Newell	N	page 68
1925	San José	136 Clayton Ave	House	Brown, Clinton E. & Elizabeth	Pogue, William	Y	page 127
1925	San José	32 E Humboldt St	House	Brown, Jerome C. & Eileen	Paskie, F.C.	Y	
1925	San José	1120 S Ninth St	House	Cambiano, Joe	Saserta, John	Y	
1925	San José	361 W Santa Clara St	Garage	Close & Close	Jorgensen, Peter	N	page 127
1925	San José	1395 Yosemite Ave	House	Close, William Jr. & Irba		Y	page 127
1925	San José	166 W San Fernando St	Laundry	Cortere, Marie & Jean	Compton, Al	N	
1925	San José	Orvis Ave near S Twelfth St	House	Crosby Brothers		N	
1925	San José	Almaden Rd & Vine St	Warehouse	De Rochebrune, Julia D.	Cooke, C.W.	N	
1925	San José	545 S Fourteenth St	House	Dorr, Harvey E. & Stella		Y	page 128

Year	City	Address	Project	Owner	Builder	Extant	See
1925	San José	Almaden Rd & Vine St	Warehouse	Dorrance, John P.		N	
1925	San José	114 E Santa Clara St	Commercial addition	Fox, Edward	Field, Z.O.	Y	
1925	San José	777 E William St	House	Friend, George C. & Mary	Keesling, Charles F.	Y	page 130
1925	San José	570 E San Carlos St	House	Grey, Herbert E. & Doris		Y	page 131
1925	San José	190 N Thirteenth St	House remodel	Hobson, Herman W.	Cooke, C.W.	Y	
1925	San José	1056 University Ave	House	Hulse, George E.		N	
1925	San José	656 S Thirteenth St	House	Jones, Alfred & Elmi	Jones, Alfred	Y	page 131
1925	San José	996 S Ninth St	House	Kestler, Linnie T.	Field, Z.O.	Y	
1925	San José	45 W St. James St	Addition to garage	Letcher, Clarence H.	Jorgensen, Peter	N	
1925	San José	295 Sequoia Ave	House	Maderis, Anthony W. & Clara	Maderis, Anthony W.	Y	page 132
1925	San José		House	Masel, Joseph G. & Estelle		Unk	
1925	San José	696 E Empire St	House	Maxwell, William & Marie	Sherman, H.R.	Y	page 136
1925	San José	Market St betw San Fernando & Park Ave	Store	McKiernan, Joseph M.	Smith, B.J.	N	
1925	San José	152 Post St	Warehouse	Mollering & Goodwin		Y	
1925	San José	503 W Santa Clara St	Store & residence	Morella, James J. & May	Megna & Newell	N	
1925	San José		House	Mortensen, E.		Unk	
1925	San José	99 Pleasant St	Alameda French Bakery	Murillo, Basile		N	
1925	San José	208 W Santa Clara St	Commercial addition	Pascoe & Smith		N	
1925	San José	730 Palm Haven Ave	House	Potter, Arthur C. & Alice	Rossi, L.C.	Y	page 136
1925	San José	480 S Fourteenth St	House	Price, Thomas H. & Daisie	Lamb, J.E.	Y	page 141
1925	San José	1200 S Second St	House	Raggio, Peter & Santina	Keesling, Charles F.	Y	page 137
1925	San José	S First St & E Reed St	Apts & house	Romsello, W.L.		N	
1925	San José	401 N Seventeenth St	House	Roney, Frederick S. & Margaret	Thermolite Co.	Y	page 139
1925	San José	601 S First St	Stores & House addition	Saso/Sasso, M.	Bigger, W.L.	Y	
1925	San José	Market St & San Antonio	Convert bldg into armory	Scheller, Victor	Sumners, R.O.	N	
1925	San José	157 W San Fernando St	Garage	Shenk & Doyle		Y	
1925	San José	485 S Fifth St	Duplex	Sweet, Hazel	Haskins & Bowen	Y	
1925	San José	1247 S First St	Apt Bldg + stores	Tomasello, Phillip	Sherman, H.R.	Y	
1925	San José	68 S Second St	House Alterations	Wagner Bros	Perkins, James E.	N	
1925	San José	704 Palm Haven Ave	House	Wolfe, E.L. & Marie	Wolfe, E.L.	Y	page 139
1925	San José	1008 Lincoln Ave	House	Wolfe, Frank D.		Y	
1925	San Mateo	121 Tilton Ave	Apt	Adams, Charles G.	Adams, Charles G.	Y	page 126
1925	San Mateo	217 C St	House alterations	Lorado, Charles	Adams, Charles G.	Unk	
1925	San Mateo	1327 B St	House	McSweeney, Ambrose		Y	
1925	Santa Clara	Kifer Rd	House	Brown, Walter G. & Isabel		Unk	
1925	Santa Clara	989 Main St	Commercial	Rose, Dr. Louis M.		N	
1925	Saratoga	19941 Sunset Dr	House	Clayton, James B. & Olive	Lindblom, George	Y	page 143
1925	Saratoga/Los Gatos	19770 Glen Una Dr	House	Dwyer, Daniel J.		Unk	
1926	Atherton	Stockbridge Ave near Eleanor Dr	House	Brassy, Rene & Ernestine	Perkins, James E.	Unk	
1926	Hollister	911 Monterey St	House	Tebbetts, May & Dr. James H.		Y	page 144
1926	Los Gatos	Santa Cruz Ave	Lodge remodel	Crider, J. Walter		Unk	
1926	Morgan Hill	17305 Monterey Rd	Hotel	Skeels, Harry & Cynthia		N	
1926	Mountain View	241 Castro	Telephone bldg	Pacific Telephone & Telegraph		Y	

Year	City	Address	Project	Owner	Builder	Extant	See
1926	San José	1287 University Ave	House	Alexander, A. Clyde & Elise		Y	page 140
1926	San José	396 N First St	Office & storage bldg alterations	Borchers Bros.		Y	page 140
1926	San José	Miller St & Asbury St	House	Budlong, Emma	Miller, Harry	N	
1926	San José	771 N Second St	House	Carrozza, Ralph & Louise	Johnson & Rodriguez	Y	
1926	San José	451 Stockton St	Store & residence	Dorsett, Percy F.	Cooke, C.W.	N	
1926	San José	813 N Second St	House	Fehren, Frederick G.	Perkins, James E.	Y	
1926	San José	305 S Tenth St	Duplex	Fleming, Charles J.	Johnson & Rodriguez	N	
1926	San José	Race St & Moorpark Ave	Warehouse & office	Foster brothers		N	
1926	San José	663 N San Pedro St	House	Fratangelo, Charles		Y	
1926	San José	210 E Julian St	Duplex	Halloran, Philip J.	Waltz, Howard	Y	page 141
1926	San José	624 S Fourteenth St	House	Jones, Alfred	Jones, Alfred	Y	
1926	San José	Fourth St near St. John St	Commercial	Jorgensen, R.		N	
1926	San José	Second St & Fountain Alley	Commercial bldg	Marchese, John		N	
1926	San José	230 First St	Garage alterations	Osen Motor Sales		N	
1926	San José	S Fourth St near E San Salvador St	House	Phillips, Hannah	Waltz, Howard	N	
1926	San José	2056 Alameda Way	House	Price, Thomas H. & Daisie		Y	page 141
1926	San José	39 N Fifth St	Apt bldg conversion	Steindorf, Miss S.	Miller, Harry	N	
1926	San José	Race St & Moorpark Ave	Cannery	United States Products Co.	Butcher, Roy M.	N	
1926	San José	935 Riverside Dr	House	Wolfe, Carl	Ouimet, Benjamin	Y	page 146
1926	Saratoga	19518 Glen Una Dr	House	Rankin, Maurice J. & Madeline	Lindblom, George	Y	page 142
1927	Burlingame	720 Newhall Rd	House	Aldrich, William		Y	
1927	Hollister	610-628 San Benito St	Store addition	Ladd, Louis		Y	
1927	Hollister	680 College St	Residence	Sacred Heart Convent	Miller, E.F., Megna & Newell	Y	page 152
1927	Hollister		School	Sacred Heart Convent	Miller, E.F.	Y	page 152
1927	Los Gatos		House	Bergman, C.A.	Allison, R.W.	Unk	
1927	Los Gatos	Marienwood	House	Shaner, George		Unk	
1927	Salinas	525 Pajaro St	House	Appleby, Dr. Ray & Florence	McCrary, Fred	Y	
1927	San José	White Rd	House	Alario, A.	Spotswood, G.W.	Unk	
1927	San José	94 S Second St	Store alterations	Blanchard, Marcus		N	
1927	San José	220-230 W Santa Clara St	Auto Showroom	Campen, Fritz (Normandin & Campen)	Swensen, Carl	N	
1927	San José	The Alameda	Stores	Cooper-Challin		Unk	
1927	San José	1328 Emory St	House	Cox, Frank Jr.	Rossi, L.C.	Y	page 149
1927	San José		House	Curry, C.W.	Gray, Robert	Unk	
1927	San José		House	Elvarado, Harvey		Unk	
1927	San José	1611 The Alameda	House	Goldeen, Edith & Joseph	Teigland, C.	Y	page 149
1927	San José	501 Stockton Ave	Duplex	Gottenberg, Emmet & Mabel	Berg, N.O.	Y	page 150
1927	San José	W Santa Clara St	50ft frontage	Hart, Alex J.		N	
1927	San José	380 W William St	2-story apts & garage	Heple, Marguerite	Morrison Brothers	N	
1927	San José	1161 Glenn Ave	House	Knollin, Ernesto R.		Y	
1927	San José	421 E Santa Clara St	Apt Bldg	LiCursi, Salvatore	Maggio, Vincent	Y	page 151
1927	San José	417 S First St	Store	Parkinson, A. Leroy	Summers, R.O.	Y	
1927	San José	948 E Santa Clara St	Commercial	Polissar, Joseph	Cooke, C.W.	Y	page 151
1927	San José	15 S Twentieth St	House	Polissar, Joseph & Bluma	Cooke, C.W.	Y	page 151
1927	San José	525 W St. John St	Foundry	San José Foundry	Persy, Frank	Y	

Year	City	Address	Project	Owner	Builder	Extant	See
1927	San José	755/759 Riverside Dr	Duplex	Silva, Marian V.	Miller, Harry	Y	page 154
1927	San José	605 S Fifteenth St	House	Smith, Christopher & Mary	Ouimet, Benjamin	Y	page 154
1927	San José	44 S Eleventh St	House remodel	Speaker, John & Martha	Jones, Alfred	Y	
1927	San José		House	Strange, Carl & Louise	Greene, W.P.	Unk	
1927	San José	1154 Glenn Ave	House	Williams, John S. Jr & Mildred	Jones, Alfred	Y	page 155
1927	Sunnyvale		School	Sunnyvale School System		N	
1928	Hollister	848 Monterey St	House remodel	Shaw, Robert		Y	
1928	Milpitas		House	Thorsen, William		Unk	
1928	Monterey	280 Alvarado St	Commercial	Pryor, John P.	Coon, H.D.	N	
1928	Pittsburg	501 York St	Store & Apts	Gambino, Phillip		N	
1928	San José	1681 The Alameda	Apt complex	Atlas, Morris		Y	page 156
1928	San José	1845 The Alameda	House	Bigley, Charles & Mary	Perkins, James E.	Y	page 156
1928	San José	59 S Claremont Ave	House	Estrem, William C.	Anderson, Paul	Y	
1928	San José	S Second St	Commercial Alterations	Gairaud, Louis		Unk	
1928	San José	460 N First St	Mission Court Apts	Hobson & Beal	Tynan Lumber	Y	page 161
1928	San José	16 W San Salvador St	Commercial	McVey, Rowena	Hathaway, E.A.	N	
1928	San José	943 Riverside Dr	House	Murray, Marie	Wolfe, E.L.	Y	
1928	San José	Alviso Rd	2 story 8 rm House	Name withheld		Unk	
1928	San José	Keyes & S. Eighth St	House	Neves, Frank		N	
1928	San José	761 Pershing Ave	House	Perry, Frank	Brotzman, Ira	Y	page 162
1928	San José	1295 Randol Ave	House	Peters, Woodie J. & Mava	Bailey, W.E.	Y	page 164
1928	San José	247 E St. John St	Auto shop	Plat, Gaston	Keesling, Charles F.	Y	page 164
1928	San José	21 S Market St	Stores & Apts Alterations	Rampone, Romolo & Co	Collison & Baker	N	
1928	San José	1275 Randol Ave	House	Schmidt, John J. & Dolly	Herschbach & Carrino, S.	Y	
1928	San José	5498 McKee Rd	House	Williams, Amos O. & Minnie	McWilliams, John	Y	page 165
1928	San José	596 S Thirteenth St	House	Wilson, Fred S. & Charlotte	Van Dalsem, Volney L.	Y	page 168
1928	San Mateo	232 Harvard Rd	House	Casey, William W. & Louise	Ferrea, Frank	Y	page 160
1928	San Mateo		House	Taylor, Harold		Unk	
1929	Kings Mountain	Unk	House	Kardos, Emil		Unk	
1929	Los Altos		House	Tisdale, P.M.		Unk	
1929	Los Gatos		House	Rodehaver, George W.	Osborne, J.W. & Knight, R.C.	Unk	
1929	San José	East Highlands, Lot 63	House	Abbott, William J. & Louise	McLean Bros.	Unk	
1929	San José	865 The Alameda	Garage	Bigley, Charles	Rossi, L.C.	N	
1929	San José	1895 Park Ave	House remodel	Burrell, Frank L. & Ann	Maurer, Carl C.	N	
1929	San José	976 Asbury St	House	Cerruti, Leland & Lorine	Keesling, Charles F.	Y	page 170
1929	San José	865 The Alameda	Auto showroom	Leland Cerruti Co.	Rossi, L.C.	Y	page 170
1929	San José	955 Willow Glen Way	House	Close, Allen & Cecelia		Y	
1929	San José	914 N First St	House	Devers, John N. & Alma	Sinnett, George	N	
1929	San José	675 S Fifteenth St	House	Emerson. Frankie		Y	
1929	San José	Ridgeview Ave	House	Hansen, Floyd & Mabel	Latta, Guy M.	Unk	
1929	San José	625 Morse St	House	Kane, Charles & Mary	Ouimet, Benjamin	Y	page 173
1929	San José	601 N Sixteenth St	House	Levin, Dan & Helen	Robinson, Ed	Y	
1929	San José	Park Ave & Naglee Ave	Store	Mise, John S.	Smith, B.J. & Sides, W.W	N	
1929	San José	The Alameda near N Morrison Ave	Store	Pollard, Thomas	Darrah, Neil	N	page 116
1929	San José	1116 Minnesota Ave	House addition	Saunders, Dr. Clark	Rossi, L.C.	N	

Year	City	Address	Project	Owner	Builder	Extant	See
1929	San José	1342 Lincoln Ave	City hall & firehouse	Willow Glen	Bridges, H.A.	Y	
1929	San José	454 Snyder Ave	House	Wolfe, Carl		Y	
1929	San José	75 S Eleventh St	Woman's club	San José Woman's Club	Neves, Frank	Y	page 176
1929	Santa Clara	Reed St & Lawrence Expwy	School	Jefferson Union School District	Swanson, Carl	N	page 191
1930	Hayward	Hesperian Blvd & Bay Bridge Blvd	House	Dennis, Robin W.	Asmussen, George J.	N	
1930	Hollister	620 Monterey St	Church alterations	Presbyterian Church		Y	
1930	San José	347 N Ninth St	House	Ariente, Gayton & Lillian	Leone, G.	Y	
1930	San José	150 N Twenty-sixth St	House	Besecker, William H. & Martha	Painter, B.H.	Y	
1930	San José	1863 Lincoln Ave	House	Blase, Anthony A. & Lydia	Maderis, Anthony W.	Y	page 178
1930	San José	581 S Thirteenth St	House	Blockie, Gus & Maude	Waltz, Howard	Y	page 179
1930	San José	Willow Glen	Store	Brown, Guy W.	Brown, Guy W.	Unk	
1930	San José		Museum	California Pioneers of Santa Clara County		NA	
1930	San José	586 S Thirteenth St	House	Callahan, Thomas J. & Edna	Keesling, Charles F.	Y	page 181
1930	San José	Alum Rock Ave.	House	Clare, Arthur & Rosa	Clare, Arthur	Unk	
1930	San José	1180 Mariposa Ave	House	Clare, Arthur & Rosa	Clare, Arthur	Y	page 183
1930	San José	295 W San Carlos St	Hester Dairy	Haas, Martin	Thorp, J.C.	N	page 186
1930	San José	595 S Sixteenth St	House	Harlan, Orren A & Alma	Neves, Frank	Y	
1930	San José	Delmas Ave near William St	Houses (2)	Herschbach, Thomas H.	Herschbach, T.H.	N	
1930	San José	1251 Yosemite Ave	House alterations	Kneeshaw, Dr. Stanley R. & Marie	DiFiore, F.	Y	page 62
1930	San José		House	Locke, E.	Waltz, Howard	Unk	
1930	San José	1963 Lincoln Ave	House	Maderis, Anthony W.		Y	
1930	San José	Silver Creek Rd	House	Pfeffer, William	Perkins, James E.	Unk	
1930	San José	425 S Market St	Auto Showroom	Pichetti Bros.		N	page 56
1930	San José	Quito Rd near Saratoga	House	Prosetti, L.H.	Keesling, Charles F.	Unk	
1930	San José	42-44 Race St	Dairy	Rossi, Luther C.	Rossi, L.C.	Y	
1930	San José	75 N Third St	Lodge	Slovonian Hall	Neves, Frank	N	
1930	San José	516 Senter Rd	House	Swickard, John A. & Evelyn		N	
1930	San José	1005 Willow Glen Way	House	Van Dalsem, Volney L.	Van Dalsem, Volney L.	Y	page 186
1930	San José		School	Willow Glen School	Anderson, Paul	N	
1930	San José	Evergreen	House	Withheld		Unk	
1930	San José	645 Palm Haven Ave	House	Wolfe, E.L.		Y	page 187
1930	Santa Clara	1060 Franklin St	Store	George, Joseph T.		N	
1930	Santa Clara	Franklin St	Store alterations	Machefert, Belle	Neves, Frank	N	
1930	Santa Clara		House	Morrison, A.R.		Unk	
1930	Santa Clara	1048 Franklin St	Creamery	Santa Clara Creamery (V.M. Kane)		N	
1930	Watsonville		3-story Apts & garage	Thompson, Stewart		Unk	
1931	Burlingame	1341 Paloma Ave	House	Hargrave, Edmond J. & Mary	Hargrave, E.J.	Y	page 190
1931	Oakland		House	Harrell, G.E.		Unk	
1931	San José	633 Auzerais Ave	Store & Apts	Albanese, Rocco		N	
1931	San José	1553 Bird Ave	House	Buchser, Emil & Neola	Herschbach, Robert	Y	page 188
1931	San José		Houses (3)	Chute, Mary		Unk	
1931	San José	84 N First St	Store	Cimino Bros.	Maggio, Vincent	Y	
1931	San José	1001 Delmas Ave	Store & House	Della Maggiore, Dario	Giacolone	Y	page 189
1931	San José	101 Keyes St	Office bldg	Gladding Bros. Mfg. Co.	Keesling, Charles F.	Y	page 189

Year	City	Address	Project	Owner	Builder	Extant	See
1931	San José	967 Riverside Dr	House	Graham, Herschel C. & Mildred	Goldstein, Adolph	Y	page 190
1931	San José	W Julian St & N San Pedro	store	Hayden, John	Caldwell, W.M.	N	
1931	San José	1425 Naglee Ave	Duplex	Mise, John S.		N	
1931	San José	Enchanto Vista Dr	House	Muetze, Paul & Grace	Keesling, Charles F.	Unk	
1931	San José	68 E Mission St	House	Walsh, William	DiFiore, Sano	Y	
1931	San José	Willow Glen	School	Willow Glen School	Nielsen, N.J.	N	
1931	Santa Clara		Store & offices	Sims, Eugene		Unk	
1931	Saratoga	Monte Vista Dr	Store	Rifredi, Charles		N	
1931	St. Helena	1325 Adams St	School	St. Helena School District		Y	page 191

Bibliography

Abbott, Carl. *How Cities Won the West: Four Centuries of Urban Change in Western North America.* Albuquerque: University of New Mexico Press, 2008.

Adams, Marian Leib. "624 Mayfield Avenue." *Historic Houses VI: Lower San Juan Neighborhood, Continued.* Stanford: Stanford Historical Society, 2012.

Archives & Architecture, LLC. State of California Department of Parks and Recreation Primary Record. "Wilmer and Dorothy Gross House." Recorded 2015.

Baker, John Milnes. *American House Styles: A Concise Guide.* W.W. Norton & Company, 1994.

Balboa Park, "History," accessed December 9, 2016, http://www.balboapark.org/info/history.

"Bill Higgins," *Mercury News Online,* accessed December 9, 2016, http://www.legacy.com/obituaries/mercurynews/obituary.aspx?n=bill-higgins&pid=20177836&.

Borbely, Michael, and Brian Hoffman. *Images of America: Palm Haven.* Charleston: Arcadia Publishing, 2013.

Brey, Karen. *Images of America: Campbell,* Arcadia Publishing, 2004.

"Building Boom is Looked for in this City." *The Evening News.* January 30, 1919.

"Building the Conservatory of Music," *The Evening News,* January 8, 1918.

"Building Will Set Record in 1922 is Belief." *The Evening News,* December 31, 1921.

"California Bricks," accessed December 9, 2016, https://calbricks.netfirms.com/brick.pk.html.

"Carl J. Wolfe Answers Call," *San Jose Mercury Herald,* July 4, 1931.

Cerny, Susan Dinkelspiel. *An Architectural Guidebook to San Francisco and the Bay Area.* Gibbs Smith, 2007.

"Clarence H. Letcher to Build his Third Garage," *Sunday Mercury and Herald,* September 29, 1907.

Clark, Shannon E. *The Alameda: The Beautiful Way.* Alameda Business Association, 2006.

"Compact Small Home Combines Conveniences," *San Jose Mercury Herald,* October 23, 1926.

"Construction of the Davis Home to Start," *San Jose Mercury Herald,* March 26, 1915.

Cook, S.F. "Jerry" III, and Skinner, Tina. *Spanish Revival Architecture.* Pennsylvania: Schiffer Publishing Ltd., 2005.

Curl, James Stevens. Encyclopaedia of Architectural Terms. UK: Donhead Publishing Ltd. Reprint 1997.

David, Leslie, "Julia Bolado Ashe Davis," accessed May 15, 2016, https://benitolink.com/legacy-women-julia-bolado-ashe-davis.

Davis, Ellis A. ed. *Davis' Commercial Encyclopedia of the Pacific Southwest.* Oakland, CA: 1918.

"Dr. Nims has Won His Suit," *San Jose Evening News,* April 13, 1906.

"Doctors Must Answer for Cunningham Murder," *Santa Cruz Evening Sentinel,* July 20, 1905.

"Domestic Architecture that is Different." *The Architect and Engineer,* February, 1914.

Doten, Alfred. *The Journals of Alfred Doten.* University of Nevada Press, 1975.

"Dreischmeyer is Sentenced to a Five Year Term," *San Jose Evening News,* June 27, 1913.

"Dreischmeyer Pleads Guilty to Embezzlement," *San Jose Evening News,* June 20, 1913.

"Eight Years in San Quentin for Dreischmeyer" *San Jose Evening News,* June 23, 1913.

Espinola, George. *Cottages, Flats, Buildings & Bungalows: 102 Designs from Wolfe & McKenzie 1907.* Bay and Valley Publishers, 2004.

"Father, Girl, Parted 18 Years Ago, Meet Here After War Horrors." *San Jose Evening News,* October 13, 1922.

"Flat Surfaces Made Artistic in Wright Home," *San Jose Mercury Herald,* October 9, 1926.

"Former Santa Clara Girl Makes Hit in Vaudeville as Barefoot Dancer," San Francisco Chronicle, October 20, 1912.

"Frank Deischmeyer Held to Answer for Embezzlement," *San Jose Evening News,* June 18, 1913.

Freitas, Melanie Shaffer. *Venetian Court, Est 1924: Capitola's Unique & Charming Seaside Resort.* 2006.

"Fruit Industry Making Giant Strides in San Benito County," *San Jose Mercury Herald,* February 19, 1921.

Fullerton Heritage, "Bungalow Courts," accessed December 9, 2016, http://www.fullertonheritage.org/Resources/archstyles/bungalow.htm.

Gage, M.D. "Scarcely any Two of the Many New Residences in Naglee Park are of Same Identical Design." *Sunday Mercury and Herald,* December 18, 1904.

Gebhard, Patricia. *George Washington Smith: Architect of the Spanish-Colonial Revival*. Gibbs Smith; 1St Edition 2005.

Gellner, Arrol, and Keister, Douglas. *Red Tile Style: America's Spanish Revival Architecture*, Avery Pub Group, 2002.

Giarratana, Elizabeth. *Old Willow Glen: A Photographic Sketchbook*. Fifth Printing. Sunnyvale: Consolidated Publications, Inc. 1988.

Goodhue, Bertam G. "The Buildings for the Panama-California Exposition San Diego, California," *Architectural Review*, April, 1914.

Gottschalk, Mary. "Oldest building at Bellarmine boasts long history in San Jose neighborhood," August 12, 2010, The Mercury News Online, accessed July 12, 2016, http://www.mercurynews.com/almaden/ci_15763294.

Grapentine, Bryan. "The Virginia City, Nevada Ink Bottles of R.L. Higgins." *Bottles and Extras*, Spring 2003.

Gregory, James N. "The Shaping of California History," accessed December 9, 2016, http://faculty.washington.edu/gregoryj/California%20History.htm.

Herhold, Scott, "Ambulances once raced to the scene in San Jose," *The Mercury News*, October 2, 2010.

Historic American Buildings Survey (Library of Congress), *Hanchett Residence Park, 1225-1257 Martin Avenue, San Jose, Santa Clara County, CA*. HABS CAL,43-SANJOS,8-, 1979.

"Housing Shortage Becoming Serious." *San Jose Mercury Herald*, August 17, 1920.

History Detectives, "Episode 6, 2003: John Brown Letters," accessed July 28, 2016, http://www-tc.pbs.org/opb/historydetectives/static/media/transcripts/2011-05-07/106_johnbrownletters.pdf

Holabird, Fred N. "The Original Higgins Ink: A Nevada Invention," *Bottles and Extras,* Spring 2003.

"Housing Shortage Becoming Serious." *San Jose Mercury Herald*, August 17, 1920:

James, Ronald, and James, Susan, *A Short History of Virginia City*. University of Nevada Press, 2014.

Kent, William Winthrop. "Domestic Architecture of California: III Part Illustrating the Influence of the Spanish and Italian Renaissance." *Architectural Forum* April 1920.

"Last Rites for F. D. Wolfe Held." *San Jose Mercury*, August 19, 1926.

Lewis, Betty, *W.H. Weeks: Architect*, Fresno: Pioneer Publishing Co., 1985.

Lichtenstein, Bea. *Images of America: Santa Clara*. Arcadia Publishing, 2004.

McAlester, Virginia Savage. *A Field Guide to American Houses: The Definitive Guide to Identifying and Understanding America's Domestic Architecture*. Second edition. Knopf, 2013.

"Miss Alice Bassler to Study in Europe," *Sunday Mercury and Herald*, June 23, 1912.

"The Mirassou Legacy," accessed December 9, 2016, http://www.mirassou.com/history.

"Mission Court History" accessed September 7, 2016, http://www.oocities.org/mission_court_apts/history.htm.

"Naglee Park Tract," *San Jose Mercury*, May 4, 1902.

"New School Building," *St. Helena Star*, June 17, 1932.

"Palm Haven," accessed December 20, 2016. www.palmhaven.info

PAST Consultants, LLC, *San José Modernism Historic Context Statement*, 2009.

Phillips, Steven J. *Old-House Dictionary: An Illustrated Guide to American Domestic Architecture*. Preservation Press, 1994.

Pratt, Constance. "675 Alvarado Row," *Historic Houses II: Lower San Juan District,* Stanford: Stanford Historical Society, 1998.

"Prominent Santa Clara Woman dies," *San Jose Evening News,* February 15, 1918.

"Prosecution of a San Jose Doctor," *The Evening News*, July 19, 1905.

Raiguel, W.O. ,"Tile Roofs," *The Architect & Engineer,* April 1923.

"R.L. Higgins Took Poison By Mistake." *San Jose Evening News*, January 25, 1905.

St. Helena Elementary School. St. Helena Historic Resources Inventory.

"Salinas and Hollister, Centers of Rich Counties," *Sunday Mercury and Herald,* April 21, 1907.

"San Jose Investors to Erect Forty-Six Venetian Court Bungalows at Capitola" *Santa Cruz News*, February 11, 1924.

"San Jose Woman's Club," accessed December 9, 2016, http://www.sjwomansclub.org/history.html.

"Santa Clara Woman's Club Played Key Role in Getting Vote for Women," accessed December 9, 2016, http://www.santaclaraweekly.com/2011/Issue-41/santa_clara_womans_club_played_key_role_in_getting_vote_for_women_in_1911.html.

Sawyer, Eugene. *History of Santa Clara County*. Los Angeles: Historic Record Company, 1922.

"School Trustees Call Bond Election and Set Date for Tuesday, April 21st," *St. Helena Star,* March 27, 1931.

Schmucker, Kristine. "The Most Complete and Convenient Court House in the State: Harvey County's First Courthouse," accessed June 7, 2016, http://hchm.org/tag/william-l-ross.

Sourisseau Academy for State and Local History, *Guide to the Charles B. Polhemus Family Albums*, 1886-1924, accessed July 12, 2016, http://www.oac.cdlib.org/findaid/ark:/13030/kt909nf85q/entire_text/.

"Spanish-California Home Possesses Spirit of West," *San Jose Mercury Herald*, October 16, 1926.

"Spanish Residence to Be Built Here," *San Jose Mercury Herald*, January 2, 1921:14.

Thornton, Rosemary and Wolicki, Dale Patrick. *California's Kit Homes: A Reprint of the 1925 Pacific Ready-Cut Homes Catalog.* Alton, IL: Gentle Beam Publications, 2004.

"Two Doctors Charged with Murder of a Young Girl," *The San Francisco Call*, July 19, 1905.

Van Laan, Krista. *Frank Delos Wolfe: California Prairie Architecture*, San José: Archives & Architecture, 2014.

"Venetian Court, Capitola By the Sea, Being Built to House Visitors," *Santa Cruz Evening News*, April 29, 1924.

"Was Unselfish Friend of Unfortunate Girl," *Sunday Mercury and Herald*, November 19, 1905.

Weinstein, Dave, and Linda Svendsen. *Signature Architects of San Francisco Bay Area.* Gibbs Smith, 2006.

"Why the Local Schools Must Be Enlarged," *San Jose Evening News*, March 3, 1920.

"Wife of Clarence Letcher Shoots Him, Kills Self," *San Jose Mercury Herald*, July 3, 1926.

Willow Glen Neighborhood Association. *Touring Historic Willow Glen: Ten Walking Loops.* Second Printing. San Jose: National Trust for Historic Preservation, 2008.

"Win the War First, says Expert Here," *The Evening News*, October 23, 1918.

Winslow, Carleton Monroe. *The Architecture and the Gardens of the San Diego Exposition*, San Francisco: Paul Elder and Co. Publishers, 1916.

Winter, Robert. *Batchelder Tilemaker,* Los Angeles: Balcony Press, 1999.

"Woman's Club of Santa Clara will fill it with Relics of Old Mission Days," *San Jose Mercury Herald*, July 22, 1914.

Woolacott, Angela, Pursell, Carroll, with Myer, Chuck. *Gilroy's Old City Hall.* Cupertino: California History Center and Foundation, 1991.

"Work Begins Upon Venetian Court at Capitola Beach," *Santa Cruz News*, March 25, 1924.

The information in this book came from a combination of reference materials in addition to those cited in this bibliography. As no business records of Wolfe & Higgins are known to have survived, all of the buildings and building projects referenced in this book have been checked against all possible documentation, including listings in the local trade magazines and newspapers listed below. Names and dates of the buildings and their owners as well as information about the owners are gathered from city directories and census reports found on ancestry.com and in the California Room of the San José Public Library, as well as from newspapers. Additional information on San José City Landmarks can be found in documentation filed with the City Landmarks Commission. The following sources were used regularly and continuously:

The Architect and Engineer of California. San Francisco and Los Angeles, California. All issues from 1906-1931.

Building and Engineering News. San Francisco and Oakland, California. All issues from 1917-1936.

Polk-Husted City Directory Co's San Jose City and Santa Clara County Directories.

San Jose Mercury Herald and *Evening News*. 1912-1931.

www.ancestry.com.

Notes

Page 22, paragraph 4. "Spanish Residence to Be Built Here." San Jose Mercury Herald, January 2, 1922

Page 25-36: The biographical information about Frank Wolfe and his family is derived from *Frank Delos Wolfe: California Prairie Architecture.*

Page 25, paragraph 1: The eight Frank Wolfe structures on the National Register of Historic Places are:

Griffin, Willard, House and Carriage House, 12345 S. El Monte Ave. Los Altos, CA. 1901.

Old City Hall, 7410 Monterey St., Gilroy, CA. 1904.

Wilson House, 860 University St. Palo Alto, CA. 1906.

Shoup, Paul, House, 500 University Ave. Los Altos, CA. 1910.

Miller-Melone Ranch, 12795 Saratoga-Sunnyvale Rd. Saratoga, CA 1911.

Woodhills, South of Cupertino on Prospect Rd. Cupertino, CA. 1914.

Milpitas Grammar School, 160 N. Main St. Milpitas, CA. 1915.

Venetian Court Apartments, 1500 Wharf Rd. Capitola, CA. 1924.

Page 26, paragraph 2: The picture purported to be the William Ross courthouse shown in *Frank Delos Wolfe: California Prairie Architecture* was incorrect. That picture was of the 1906 courthouse building that replaced the Bretch Brothers' building, which was always intended to be used as a temporary courthouse. The Bretch Brothers' building designed by William Ross was demolished in 1994. (http://hchm.org/tag/bretch-bros/, Harvey County Historical Museum.)

Page 29, paragraph 3: Espinola, George. *Cottages, Flats, Buildings & Bungalows: 102 Designs from Wolfe & McKenzie 1907.* Pages 5-6.

Page 30, paragraph 6: In the National Register nomination, the Old Gilroy City Hall building is identified as the work of San Francisco architect Samuel Newsom "working with Wolfe & McKenzie." Local historians and additional research by this author have determined that in fact Wolfe & McKenzie were the only architects, and there is no documentation associating Newsom with the design of the building. (Woolacott, Angela, Pursell, Carroll, with Myer, Chuck. *Gilroy's Old City Hall*). Further research included reviewing many articles in the Gilroy newspapers and consulting material at the Gilroy Museum with the help of Museum volunteer Tom Howard.

Page 36, photograph top: Casa Grande, the Bolado-Davis house, has been attributed to San Francisco architect Lewis Hobart, probably due to the Davises' friendship with Hobart. Articles in the *San Jose Mercury Herald* (March 26, 1915) and the *Hollister Evening*

Free Lance (March 24, 1915) and analysis of the interior and exterior of the house all support the fact that Frank Wolfe was the architect.

Page 37, paragraph 3 and 4: Conversation with Jane Higgins Hauser, June 26, 2015. Louisa and William Smith's trip by ox team from Illinois to California is corroborated by census reports, which document their stop in Missouri where their son was born, and a February 15, 1918 obituary in the *San Jose Mercury Herald* for Martha Seydel, called the "adopted daughter" of William and Louisa Smith. She made the trip from Missouri with the Smiths at the age of thirteen.

Page 38, caption: The transcript of the *History Detectives* program can be found at http://www-tc.pbs.org/opb/historydetectives/static/media/transcripts/2011-05-07/106_johnbrownletters.pdf (accessed July 28, 2016). The program also uncovered the fact that Lucy's mother, Louisa Harlow Smith, like Lucy herself, was involved with the suffrage movement as cited in her 1908 obituary:

Mrs. Louise Harlow Smith passed away at Santa Clara June 22nd. Mrs. Smith was a pioneer of the women's suffrage movement, and was very closely identified with its work. And because of her zeal in this direction, she became well-known over the entire state.

Pages 38-39. Holabird, Fred N. "The Original Higgins Ink: A Nevada Invention," *Bottles and Extras,* Spring 2003. The 1850 census and newspapers from Reno, Nevada, and Virginia City, as well as *Alfred Doten's Journals*, provide further information on Rufus and Lucy Higgins's time in Virginia City.

Page 39, paragraph 7: William and his sister Louise, like their mother Lucy, were both involved with music. William played the flute and performed with local orchestras in San Jose. In 1922, Higgins was chair of the Music Committee of the Industrial Exposition given by the 100 Per Cent Club. Louise Higgins was said to have been an excellent singer like her mother and her, and their performances are mentioned in society columns in the local newspapers. In 1912, Louise headlined at the Victory Theater in San Jose in a "classical Egyptian barefoot dancing act" for which she was the producer, choreographer, and star. William had a major role in the piece providing the music and he received good reviews as the flute player. The October 20, 1912 *San Francisco Chronicle* reported that Louise had returned to San José to try to persuade her brother to quit his architectural career and join her new theater troupe.

Page 40, paragraph 2: "R.L. Higgins Took Poison By Mistake." *San Jose Evening News*, January 25, 1905

Page 40, paragraph 4. There have been some statements published saying that William Higgins worked for Frank Wolfe prior to the partnership. If true, this is not substantiated anywhere. Higgins did work as a draftsman for architect William Binder in 1910 (Polk City Directory, 1910) and listed himself as an Architect in city directories starting in 1907 but there is no documented connection with Wolfe until November 1917 when the partnership was announced in the November 1917 issue of *The Architect and Engineer of California*.

Page 41, paragraph 1. Higgins received his license May 1, 1913. His verbal examination was held in San Francisco's Phelan Building and administered by some of San Francisco's most highly acclaimed architects: John Bakewell Jr. of Bakewell and Brown, Samuel Newsom, and Sylvain Schnaittacher. (Information courtesy of Vickie Mayer, Assistant Executive Officer, California Architects Board.)

Page 41, paragraph 3: Conversations with Lori Deal, July 25, 2015, who provided the photographs of the Higgins house in its three incarnations.

Pages 42-44: (Archives & Architecture, LLC. State of California Department of Parks and Recreation Primary Record. "Wilmer and Dorothy Gross House.")

Page 49, paragraph 3: Carl Wolfe's obituary (*San Jose Mercury Herald*, July 4, 1931) states that he attended Heidelberg University and the 1907 Heidelberg yearbook shows him as part of the class of 1907 and an art student.

Page 49, paragraph 3: The tragic story of Gladys Cunningham's July 17, 1905 death filled local newspapers for two months. Two doctors and a nurse were arrested after her death. Dr. Herbert Nims of San José was the Cunningham family physician who took Gladys to Dr. Thomas's clinic; he afterward claimed to know nothing of the planned abortion and suggested she may have done it to herself. In November of 1905, both he and Dr. Thomas were exonerated of all charges by San José judge Conlan, who stated that "Dr. Nims ought never to have been arrested or charge with his offense, and that as far as Dr. Thomas is concerned, the evidence shows conclusively that he is innocent of any connection with the cause which produced the girl's decease." Originally, there was a search for Carl Wolfe, who had reportedly disappeared two weeks before Cunningham's death. The July 20, 1905 issue of the *San Jose Evening News* reported that the San José police chief stated that there would be no attempt to arrest and charge Carl Wolfe. In an ironic postscript, Dr. Nims sued and won against Gladys Cunningham's father in April of 1906 for money owed him for professional services the night of the death (*San Jose Evening News*, April 13, 1906).

Page 49, paragraph 4: The construction firm of "Wolfe & Wolfe" made up of J.B. Wolfe and C.J. Wolfe advertised in Wolfe & McKenzie's *Book of Designs*. (Espinola: Page 218.)

Page 50, paragraph 6. "Carl J. Wolfe Answers Call." *San Jose Mercury Herald,* July 4, 1931.

Page 59, paragraph 2: Conversation with the owner, September 15, 2013.

Page 73, paragraph 2: Original published reports on the origin of the Taormino/Caputo house had mistakenly attributed the owners and the build date of the original house as the Frank and Viola Allen family in 1912—the Allens lived on the property next door to the Taormino property—and then to the Linegars, who had lived on the property prior to the Taorminos. Subsequent research indisputably shows that Wolfe & Higgins were commissioned by the Taorminos in 1921 as announced in several 1921 issues of *Building and Engineering News*.

Page 97, paragraph 3: Dreischmeyer's story is told in many articles in the San José newspapers in June of 1913, cited in the Bibliography.

Page 110, paragraph 2: The article "675 Alvarado Row" in *Historic Houses II: Lower San Juan District* contains the statement that the Allens had the living room nook built to accommodate the organ. However, early and revised blueprints do not show this to be the case.

Page 125: Melanie Shaffer Freitas lists the original owners' names and their unit numbers in her book Venetian Court, showing that Frank and Nellie Wolfe and the Higginses (along with Gertrude Gardiner) purchased units. Kittie Kimberlin and Henry Harms, both customers of Wolfe & Higgins, also owned units. The April 29, 1924 issue of the *Santa Cruz Evening News* lists a number of buyers not mentioned in Freitas's book, who may have been unable to complete their purchases when the plans for the remainder of the units were curtailed. Both Carl Wolfe and erstwhile Wolfe & Higgins client Tony Maderis are listed in the *Evening News* but not in Freitas's book as early buyers.

Page 132, paragraph 1: Between 1910 and 1931, Anthony Maderis commissioned first Frank Wolfe, and then Wolfe & Higgins regularly for his own residences or those he sold. (Maderis is not on record as having worked with any other architects.) In addition, Maderis probably recommended Wolfe & Higgins to many of his real estate clients—a number of Wolfe & Higgins customers, such as the Mirassous, bought land from Maderis and then commissioned plans from Wolfe & Higgins.

Page 136, paragraph 3. "Compact Small Home Combines Conveniences," *San Jose Mercury Herald*, October 23, 1926.

Page 143: "Spanish-California Home Possesses Spirit of West," *San Jose Mercury Herald*, October 16, 1926.

Page 150, paragraph 2: Maderis family stories courtesy of Judy Everett, granddaughter of Tony Maderis.

Page 152, paragraph 1: Plans for the Sacred Heart Convent were covered regularly in many 1927 issues of the *Hollister Advance*.

Page 157, paragraph 2: Wolfe & Higgins were not the only San José-based architects working heavily in the Spanish Revival style. The style was extremely popular by the late 1920s and clients who wanted fashionable houses had a wide range of excellent architects from which to choose. Several of the large 1920s residences on or near The Alameda in San José are Spanish Revival designs done by some of the leading local architects, although the Will Toepke house for Fred Cook is the only one that might be so easily mistaken for a Wolfe & Higgins. Not far from the Charles Bigley house are houses designed for Nich Scorsur by Charles McKenzie (1925), for Joseph Reiter by Ralph Wyckoff (1928), and for Richard Bressani by Herman Krause (1930). Those three architects were the serious competition for large residences in the Spanish Revival style, although none of the competitors was as prolific, nor started as early, as did Wolfe & McKenzie. Some of the local builders also worked in the Spanish Revival style without using an architect (or at least not admitting to), presumably designing and building their own houses or using kit homes from a catalog. William Lewis of San José built a number of handsome Spanish Revival homes in the Naglee Park area, including the one in which he lived with his wife Daisie, all of which, according to announcements in *Building and Engineering News*, were done without the services of an architect. A. Clyde Alexander built many Spanish Revival houses throughout San José, sometimes without the services of an architect, although he was also a regular Wolfe & Higgins client.

Page 191, paragraph 3. As early as 1930, William Weeks had announced in *Building and Engineering News* that he was working on the St. Helena High School, with an item in the March 14, 1931 issue stating that he was preparing preliminary plans. The March 21, 1931 issue contained a notice stating that he had resigned and the school board was searching for a new architect. However, the March 27, 1931 *St. Helena Star* states that the trustees had employed Wolfe & Higgins and that they had already brought drawings of the proposed building, which were "approved and admired by all who saw them." The article also stated that the Board had visited the Wolfe & Higgins Jefferson Union School several weeks prior to help them make their decision about Wolfe & Higgins.

William Weeks was an extremely well-respected architect who designed many of the best school buildings in the state of California, and in 1930 alone, he had already worked on twenty-two school and college buildings according to Weeks biographer Betty Lewis. In March of 1931, Weeks was going through serious problems. His business was under investigation for misappropriating stockholders' money and he was charged with inflating the prices of building contracts. The Board of Architectural Examiners revoked his license, but by September, the Supreme Court deemed that the Board had overstepped his bounds and Weeks got his license reinstated. The following year, he was cleared of dishonest practice. (Lewis, Betty. *W.W. Weeks, Architect.*)

Photography Credits

COVER: Krista Van Laan

PAGE 1, 23, 51, 147: Krista Van Laan

PAGE 4, 2,4 52, 148: Blueprint courtesy of San Benito County Historical Museum.

PAGES 14-17: Krista Van Laan

PAGE 18: By Carptrash (talk) ak Einar Einarsson Kvaran [CC BY-SA 3.0 (http://creativecommons.org/licenses/by-sa/3.0) or GFDL (http://www.gnu.org/copyleft/fdl.html)], via Wikimedia Commons

PAGE 19 LEFT: SOUTH (MAIN) FACADE - Balboa Park, California Tower, Balboa Park, El Prado Area, San Diego, San Diego County, CA, Reproduction Number: HABS CAL,37-SANDI,16-A--2 . Library of Congress Prints and Photographs Division Washington, D.C. 20540.

PAGE 19 RIGHT and PAGE 20 TOP RIGHT AND BOTTOM LEFT: Krista Van Laan

PAGE 20 BOTTOM RIGHT: Hayes Mansion: By Sanfranman59 - Own work, CC BY-SA 3.0, https://commons.wikimedia.org/w/index.php?curid=21684348

PAGE 21 TOP: *Architectural Forum*, April 1920

PAGE 21 BOTTOM: Hearst castle: By King of Hearts - Own work, CC BY-SA 3.0, https://commons.wikimedia.org/w/index.php?curid=21785132

PAGE 22: Krista Van Laan

PAGE 25: Courtesy of Meghan Doe Almeida

PAGE 26: Nellie Wolfe: Courtesy of John Crockett Teskey; Jeremiah Wolfe and E.L. Wolfe: Courtesy of Ann Wolfe; Carl Wolfe baby picture: Courtesy of Meghan Doe Almeida; Bretch Building: Courtesy of Harvey County Historical Museum & Archives

PAGE 27 TOP AND BOTTOM LEFT: Krista Van Laan

PAGE 27 BOTTOM RIGHT: King Conservatory of Music Catalog, 1896

PAGE 28 TOP: Charles McKenzie: Davis, Ellis A. ed. Davis' *Commercial Encyclopedia of the Pacific Southwest.* Oakland, CA: 1918

PAGE 28 CENTER: Krista Van Laan

PAGE 28 BOTTOM: Unattributed vintage postcard from the author's collection

PAGE 29 TOP LEFT: Krista Van Laan

PAGE 28 TOP RIGHT: Franklin Maggi

PAGE 28 BOTTOM: 1225 MARTIN AVENUE, SOUTHEAST FRONT - Hanchett Residence Park, 1225-1257 Martin Avenue, San Jose, Santa Clara County, CA. Library of Congress Prints and Photographs Division Washington, D.C. 20540 USA. Reproduction Number: HABS CAL,43-SANJOS,8--2

PAGE 30 TOP: South Bay Yacht Club: By Eugene Zelenko (Own work) [GFDL (http://www.gnu.org/copyleft/fdl.html) or CC BY-SA 4.0-3.0-2.5-2.0-1.0 (http://creativecommons.org/licenses/by-sa/4.0-3.0-2.5-2.0-1.0)], via Wikimedia Commons

PAGE 30 CENTER: *The Architect and Engineer*, February 1914

PAGE 30 BOTTOM: Krista Van Laan

PAGE 31: Gilroy City hall: By Sanfranman59 - Own work, CC BY-SA 3.0, https://commons.wikimedia.org/w/index.php?curid=21672513

PAGE 32 TOP LEFT: *The Architect and Engineer*, February 1914

PAGE 32 CENTER AND BOTTOM LEFT: Krista Van Laan

PAGE 32 RIGHT: Miller Melone ranch: By Sanfranman59 - Own work, CC BY-SA 3.0, https://commons.wikimedia.org/w/index.php?curid=21547201

PAGE 32 BOTTOM RIGHT: *The Architect and Engineer*, February 1914

PAGE 33: Krista Van Laan

PAGE 34 TOP LEFT: Courtesy, History San José

PAGE 34 BOTTOM LEFT and PAGE 35, TOP: Krista Van Laan

PAGE 35 RIGHT: REAR OF HOUSE, LOOKING NORTHEAST - Woodhills, Prospect Road, Cupertino, Santa Clara County, CA. Reproduction Number: HABS CAL,43-CUP,1--2. Library of Congress Prints and Photographs Division Washington, D.C. 20540.

PAGE 35 BOTTOM LEFT: *The Architect and Engineer of California*, February 1914

PAGE 36: Krista Van Laan

PAGE 37: Courtesy of Lori Deal

PAGE 38: Courtesy of Jane Higgins Hauser

PAGE 39 TOP: Courtesy of Fred Holabird

PAGE 40: Courtesy of Lori Deal

PAGE 41-42 and PAGE 43 LEFT TOP AND BOTTOM: Krista Van Laan

PAGE 43 RIGHT BOTTOM: Courtesy of Lisa and Steven Berry

PAGE 44: Krista Van Laan

PAGE 45 LEFT: Courtesy, History San José

PAGE 45 RIGHT and PAGE 46: Krista Van Laan

PAGE 47 TOP: Used with permission of San José State University Library Special Collections and Archives. From the John C. Gordon Photographic Collection, MSS-1996-03-29

PAGE 47 BELOW and PAGE 48: Krista Van Laan

PAGE 49 TOP LEFT: Courtesy of Meghan Doe Almeida

PAGE 49 BOTTOM: Krista Van Laan

PAGE 53: Photographs courtesy of the Los Gatos Library

PAGE 54 TOP LEFT: *San Jose Sunday and Mercury Herald*, September 29, 1907

PAGE 54 TOP RIGHT: Courtesy, History San José.

PAGE 54 BOTTOM LEFT: *San Jose Mercury Herald*, April 9, 1916

PAGE 55 TOP: Catherine Mills. Courtesy, History San José

PAGE 55 BOTTOM LEFT: Used with permission of San José State University Library Special Collections and Archives. From the John C. Gordon Photographic Collection, MSS-1996-03-29.

PAGE 55 BOTTOM RIGHT: *San Jose Mercury Herald*, April 9, 1916

PAGE 56 TOP RIGHT: Franklin Maggi

PAGE 56 BOTTOM: Used with permission of San José State University Library Special Collections and Archives. From the John C. Gordon Photographic Collection, MSS-1996-03-29.

PAGE 58-66: Krista Van Laan

PAGE 67: Unattributed vintage postcards from the author's collection.

PAGE 68 TOP: Krista Van Laan

PAGE 68 BOTTOM: Used with permission of San José State University Library Special Collections and Archives. From the John C. Gordon Photographic Collection, MSS-1996-03-29.

PAGE 69 TOP: Krista Van Laan

PAGE 69 BOTTOM: John Frolli, courtesy of Archives & Architecture

PAGE 70-87: Krista Van Laan

PAGE 88 TOP: Susan Farris

PAGE 88 BOTTOM and PAGE 89: Krista Van Laan

PAGE 90 LEFT: Franklin Maggi

PAGE 90 RIGHT and PAGE 91-93 and PAGE 94 TOP LEFT AND RIGHT AND BOTTOM LEFT: Krista Van Laan

PAGE 94 BOTTOM RIGHT: Franklin Maggi

PAGE 95 and PAGE 96 TOP AND LOWER RIGHT: Krista Van Laan

PAGE 96 LOWER LEFT: Used with permission of San José State University Library Special Collections and Archives. From the John C. Gordon Photographic Collection, MSS-1996-03-29.

PAGE 97-100: Krista Van Laan

PAGE 101: *The Architect and Engineer*, April 1923

PAGE 102-103: Sunny Scott

PAGE 104 and PAGE 105 LEFT TOP AND CENTER: Krista Van Laan

PAGE 105 BOTTOM RIGHT: Sharlene Van Rooy

PAGE 106 TOP: Krista Van Laan

PAGE 106 BOTTOM : Used with permission of San José State University Library Special Collections and Archives. From the John C. Gordon Photographic Collection, MSS-1996-03-29.

PAGE 107 and PAGE 108 TOP LEFT AND BOTTOM RIGHT: Krista Van Laan

PAGE 108 TOP RIGHT: Courtesy of Edith Espinola

PAGE 109-110 and PAGE 111 TOP AND BOTTOM RIGHT: Krista Van Laan

PAGE 111 BOTTOM LEFT: David Lyon. Courtesy of David Lyon and Joan Talbert.

PAGE 112-115 and PAGE 116 TOP AND RIGHT: Krista Van Laan

PAGE 116 BOTTOM LEFT AND RIGHT: Franklin Maggi

PAGE 117-121: Krista Van Laan

PAGE 122-123 BOTTOM: Franklin Maggi

PAGE 123 TOP: *Santa Cruz Evening News*, April 29, 1924.

PAGE 124-126 and PAGE 127 LEFT and BOTTOM RIGHT: Krista Van Laan

PAGE 127 TOP RIGHT: Used with permission of San José State University Library Special Collections and Archives. From the John C. Gordon Photographic Collection, MSS-1996-03-29.

PAGE 128 TOP: Krista Van Laan

PAGE 128 BOTTOM: and 129 TOP Sunny Scott

PAGE 130-133: Krista Van Laan

PAGE 134 TOP LEFT: Courtesy of Judy Everett

PAGE 134 CENTER LEFT: Courtesy of Larry Camuso

PAGE 134 BOTTOM LEFT AND RIGHT and PAGE 135: Krista Van Laan

PAGE 136: Krista Van Laan

PAGE 137 TOP LEFT: *San Jose Mercury Herald*, October 23, 1926

PAGE 137 BOTTOM-PAGE 142 and PAGE 143 TOP: Krista Van Laan

PAGE 143 BOTTOM: *San Jose Mercury Herald*, October 16, 1926

PAGE 144: Krista Van Laan

PAGE 145 TOP RIGHT: Courtesy of the San Benito County Historical Society

PAGE 145 TOP LEFT: Courtesy of Susie Alarcon

PAGE 145 BOTTOM LEFT: Sharlene Van Rooy

PAGE 145 BOTTOM RIGHT: Krista Van Laan

PAGE 146 and PAGE 149-152: Krista Van Laan

PAGE 153 TOP: Frank Van Rooy

PAGE 153 CENTER AND BOTTOM RIGHT: Krista Van Laan

PAGE 153 BOTTOM LEFT: Sharlene Van Rooy

PAGE 154-162: Krista Van Laan

PAGE 163 TOP LEFT: Courtesy of Syndi and Scott Gemmett

PAGE 163 TOP RIGHT AND BOTTOM and PAGE 164-170: Krista Van Laan

PAGE 171 TOP: Paul Dileanis, courtesy of Biggs Cardosa

PAGE 171 CENTER RIGHT: Courtesy of Biggs Cardosa

PAGE 171 BOTTOM RIGHT: Used with permission of San José State University Library Special Collections and Archives. From the John C. Gordon Photographic Collection, MSS-1996-03-29.

PAGE 171 LEFT: Krista Van Laan

PAGE 172 TOP: Krista Van Laan

PAGE 172 BOTTOM: Alvis Hendley. Courtesy of Alvis Hendley.

PAGE 173-175: Krista Van Laan

PAGE 176 TOP AND LEFT: Franklin Maggi

PAGE 176 BOTTOM RIGHT and 177 TOP: Krista Van Laan

PAGE 177 BOTTOM: Franklin Maggi

PAGE 178-185: Krista Van Laan

PAGE 186 TOP: Used with permission of San José State University Library Special Collections and Archives. From the John C. Gordon Photographic Collection, MSS-1996-03-29.

PAGE 186 BOTTOM: Krista Van Laan

PAGE 187-190 and 191 TOP: Krista Van Laan

PAGE 191 BOTTOM: Photographer unknown.

PAGE 192-197: Krista Van Laan

Index